The Elementary Calendar

By
Barbara R. Miller

Cover and Inside Illustrations by
Ronnie Walter Shipman

Publishers
Instructional Fair • TS Denison
Grand Rapids, Michigan 49544

Instructional Fair • TS Denison grants the right to the individual purchaser to reproduce patterns and student activity materials in this book for noncommercial individual or classroom use only. Reproduction for an entire school or school system is strictly prohibited. No other part of this publication may be reproduced in whole or in part. No part of this publication may be reproduced for storage in a retrieval system, or transmitted in any form or by any means, electronic, mechanical, recording, or otherwise, without the prior written permission of the publisher. For information regarding permission write to: Instructional Fair • TS Denison, P.O. Box 1650, Grand Rapids, MI 49501.

Credits
Author: Barbara R. Miller
Cover & Inside Illustrations: Ronnie Walter Shipman
Project Manager: Sherrill B. Flora
Editor: Danielle de Gregory
Art Production: Darcy Bell-Meyers
Typesetting: Deborah McNiff

About the Author
Barbara Miller is an elementary school art teacher and an exhibiting watercolorist. She is a graduate of Parsons School of Design and holds an M.A. in Art Education from New York University. Barbara and her husband, artist Russ Miller, live in Toms River, New Jersey. They have two grown children.

Standard Book Number 513-02365-8
The Elementary Calendar
Copyright © 1996 by Instructional Fair • TS Denison
2400 Turner Avenue NW
Grand Rapids, Michigan 49544

All Rights Reserved • Printed in the USA

Introduction

The Elementary Calendar for Primary Grades offers first through third grade teachers ideas, suggestions, reproducible student pages, and patterns that can be incorporated into your existing curriculum.

These instructional materials are organized by the month and are thematically-centered around special events and holidays. The practical activities and timeless teaching suggestions can be used to enrich and reinforce various subjects taught throughout the year. The content has been tried, tested and validated by teachers experienced in teaching the primary grades.

The Elementary Calendar for Primary Grades is a resource that all primary teachers will want in their libraries.

Some of the following areas are included:

- Important Birthdays of Famous People
- Art Activities
- Language Activities
- Learning Games for Health and Safety
- History and Art for Fun Social Studies Lessons
- Descriptions of Holidays from Other Lands
- Charts, Wordfinds, Crossword Puzzles
- Reproducible Calendars with Beautiful Headers
- Original Learning Poems and Stories
- And much, much, more to keep you and your students learning throughout the school year!

Table of Contents

September Contents

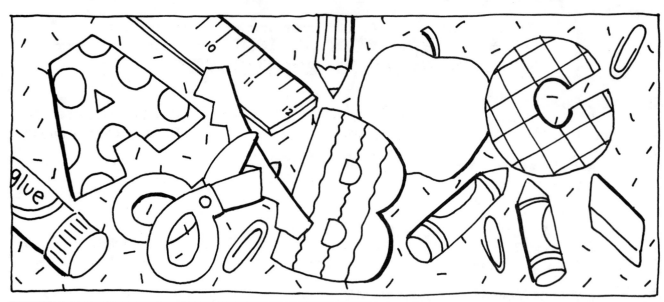

Sunday	Monday	Tuesday	Wednesday	Thursday	Friday	Saturday

September Birthdays

1	Walter Reuther	American labor leader, president of the United Auto Workers (UAW) and the Congress of Industrial Organizations (CIO)
2	Christa McAuliffe	teacher killed in Challenger explosion
4	Los Angeles	founded by decree, 1781
6	Jane Addams Marquis de Lafayette	feminist; founder of Hull House; 1931 Nobel Peace Prize French general, hero of the American Revolution
7	Grandma Moses	Anna Mary Robertson Moses, American painter who began painting at age 78
11	O. Henry	William Sydney Porter, American author
12	Jesse Owens	Olympic track and field star, 1939
15	Dame Agatha Christie William Howard Taft	British mystery writer; *Murder on the Orient Express* 27th president; chief justice Supreme Court
18	Samuel Johnson U.S. Air Force	writer; created first great English dictionary became separate service in 1947
21	H.G. Wells	Herbert George Wells, writer; *The Time Machine* and *War of the Worlds*
22	Ice cream cone	patent filed by Italo Marchiony, 1903
23	Victoria Woodhull	feminist, first female presidential candidate
24	F. Scott Fitzgerald Jim Henson	American writer; *The Great Gatsby* creator of the Muppets
26	Johnny Appleseed T.S. Eliot George Gershwin Shamu	John Chapman, naturalist; planted orchards Thomas Stearns Eliot, Anglo-American poet, playwright, critic; 1948 Nobel Prize for Literature American composer; *Rhapsody in Blue* born 1985, Sea World
27	Thomas Nast	American political cartoonist, invented elephant and donkey symbols for the Republican and Democratic parties
28	Al Capp	cartoonist, creator of Li'l Abner
30	Truman Capote	novelist, celebrity; *Breakfast at Tiffany's*

Have children draw a picture (or glue a photograph of themselves) in either of these frames for Grandparent's Day. (Also useful for Mother's Day, Father's Day, or any other Relative's Day that might be invented by the commercial greeting card industry.

TSD 2365-8 *The Elementary Calendar*

LET'S GET READY FOR SCHOOL

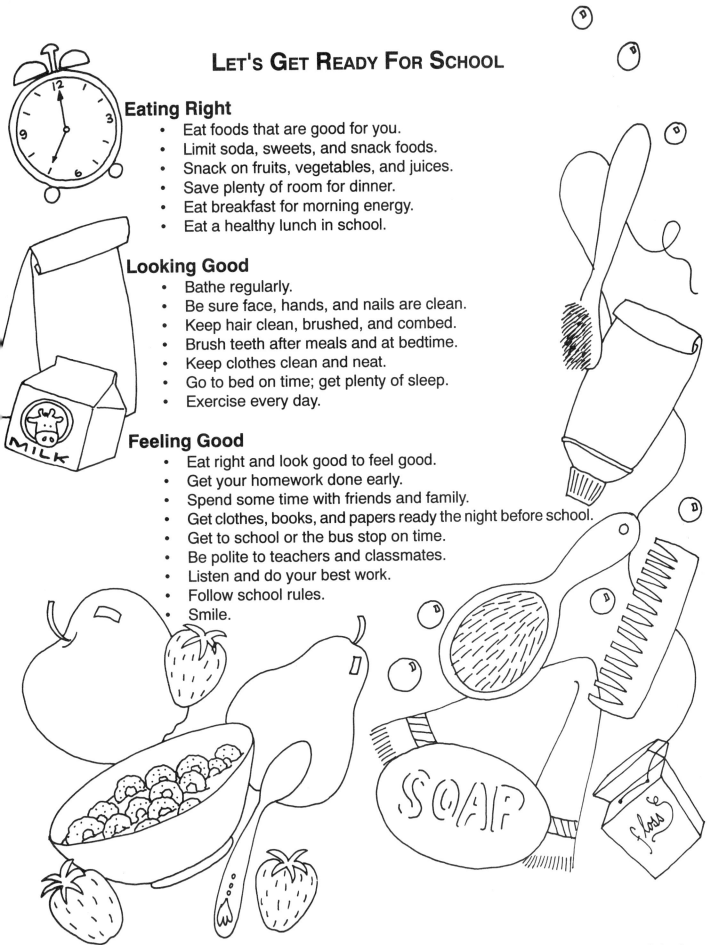

Eating Right

- Eat foods that are good for you.
- Limit soda, sweets, and snack foods.
- Snack on fruits, vegetables, and juices.
- Save plenty of room for dinner.
- Eat breakfast for morning energy.
- Eat a healthy lunch in school.

Looking Good

- Bathe regularly.
- Be sure face, hands, and nails are clean.
- Keep hair clean, brushed, and combed.
- Brush teeth after meals and at bedtime.
- Keep clothes clean and neat.
- Go to bed on time; get plenty of sleep.
- Exercise every day.

Feeling Good

- Eat right and look good to feel good.
- Get your homework done early.
- Spend some time with friends and family.
- Get clothes, books, and papers ready the night before school.
- Get to school or the bus stop on time.
- Be polite to teachers and classmates.
- Listen and do your best work.
- Follow school rules.
- Smile.

TSD 2365-8 *The Elementary Calendar*

AM I READY FOR SCHOOL?

The Night Before	M	T	W	Th	F
Did My Homework					
Clothes, Books, and Papers Are Ready for the Morning					
Took a Bath or Shower					
Brushed My Teeth					
Went to Bed on Time					
In the Morning	M	T	W	Th	F
Ate Breakfast					
Washed Hands and Face					
Brushed My Teeth					
Took a Bath or Shower					
Clothes and Hair Neat					
Prepared for Lunch					
Remembered Books and Papers					

Name: _____

Name _____

Eat Right – Look Good – Feel Good

Across

2. Get plenty of _____ at night.
4. _____ your teeth after meals.
6. Do your _____ every day.
10. Get _____; run and play.
11. Be _____ to teachers and friends.
12. _____ to what the teacher says.

Down

1. _____ your face and hands.
3. _____ your things away neatly.
4. Take a _____ or shower.
5. Put a _____ on your face.
7. _____ healthy foods.
8. _____ clothes clean and neat.
9. Obey _____ rules.

Word List: bath, brush, eat, exercise, homework, keep, listen, polite, put, school, sleep, smile, wash

Teacher: *For an easier puzzle, enter the first letter of each word before duplicating. For a harder puzzle, cover the word list as well as these suggestions when duplicating.*

GETTING READY FOR SCHOOL

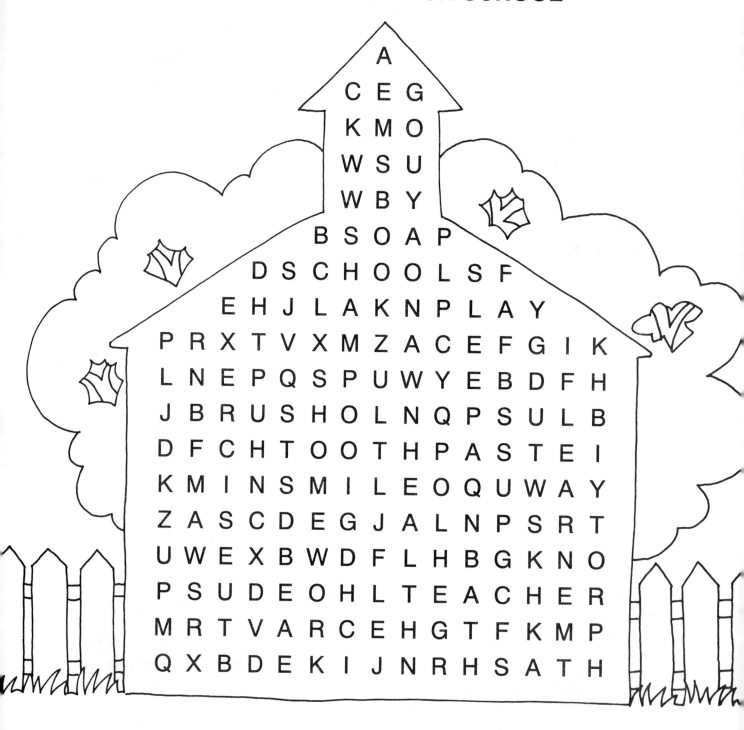

BRUSH
SOAP
TOOTHPASTE
BATH
EXERCISE

HOMEWORK
SHAMPOO
PLAY
SCHOOL
TEACHER

LEARN
SMILE
BOOK
HEALTH
SLEEP

MELISSA IS A MESS!

Help her get ready for school.

Put an "X" next to the things that will help
Melissa get ready for school. Color the pictures.

MELISSA IS ALL READY!
What else does she need for school?

Color the things that will help Melissa in school.
Put an "X" on the things that stay at home.

Name _____

Help Bonnie and Bobby walk to school. Be sure to pick up all the things they might need for school, but not the things they should leave at home. Follow the maze and color.

On the back of this paper make a list of all the things Bobby and Bonnie took to school. Underline things that you brought today as well.

15

TSD 2365-8 *The Elementary Calendar*

Alexander Earns an "A"

Now it's time for homework, my dear,
So let's just get a few things clear:

Write down your work
So you won't forget it.
Keep up in school.
You'll never regret it.

It's no one's job
To do your work for you.
Just get it all done
Before there is more due.

Here's a quiet place
You can work alone
No games or toys,
No telephone.

No radio, TV, or
Other distractions
To take your mind from
Spelling and fractions.

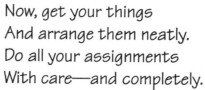

Now, get your things
And arrange them neatly.
Do all your assignments
With care—and completely.

Work done so soon?
Put it safely away,
So it's ready for school
The very next day.

Hello, Alex, dear.
What's that you say?
Why, look at that . . .
You've got an A!

TSD 2365-8 *The Elementary Calendar*

Name _____

LET'S MAKE BREAKFAST
Chose and circle food from these groups for a healthy breakfast.

Fruits & Vegetables

Cereals & Grains

OATMEAL

Milk & Dairy Products

MIL
yogurt
cottage cheese 1%
creme CHEESE

Dried Beans, Meat, Fish, Poultry, Eggs, Nuts

peanut butter

Teacher: It should be pointed out to children that 1) since they will be eating other meals, not every food group need be represented at breakfast, and 2) breakfast meats contain a great deal of fat and salt and should not be eaten often.

TSD 2365-8 *The Elementary Calendar*

```
            A D F H
        J L P N P R J T V X
    B C E G I A K M O U Q S U W
    Y A B A C O N C E F I H J L N P
    R T R V X X C O L D C E R E A L
    B D F E H J L A M O R E T V Y A C E
    E I K A M O W K S U W Y A M I L K C
    W G F K I J L E N E R G Y N P R T V
    F M U F F I N S Y A C O A T M E A L
    E H J A L N P R T U W R B L U D T S
    C I X S L R V F B T G A H K N R O U
    G J T K N O M E L O N U T C H A E
    N M S U F S C R B E G G S B T S
        O T R B R G R A P E F R U I T
        U C F D K M I O S T B C T D
        A N S U L E P R W U E S
            O E I S Z F V M N
                O D R
```

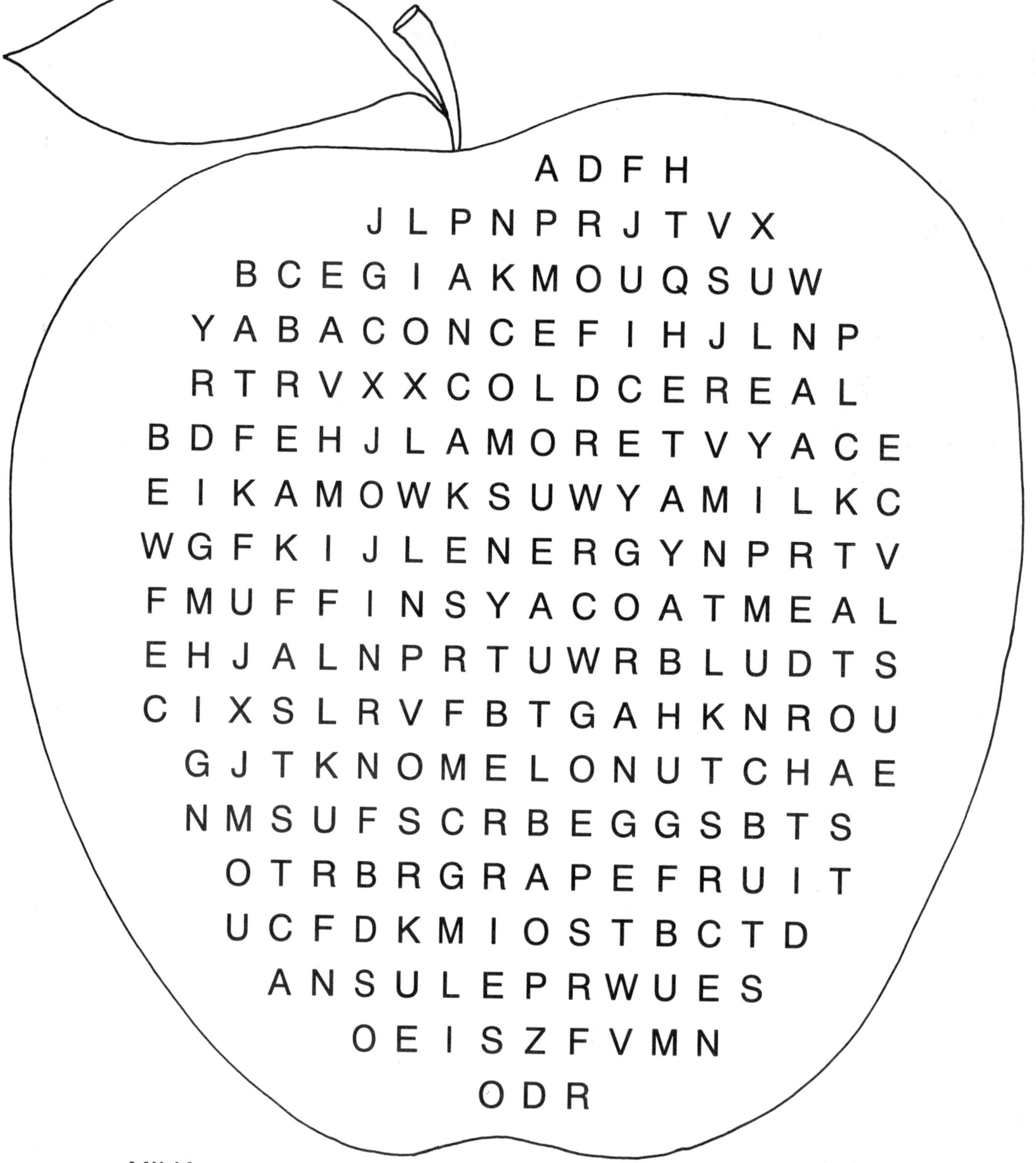

MILK
EGGS
ENERGY
BREAKFAST
PANCAKES
COLD CEREAL

BACON
MUFFINS
JUICE

TOAST
MELON
ORANGE
OATMEAL
BERRIES
GRAPEFRUIT

6

I am polite to others.

8

And I . . . .

3

I stay in my seat.

1

My book of SCHOOL RULES

TSD 2365-8 *The Elementary Calendar*

7

5

I obey playground rules.

I care for school property.

— Fold

Copy both sides on a single sheet. Cut on broken lines. Assemble and staple.

Fold —

I raise my hand to speak.

I listen and follow directions.

2

4

TSD 2365-8 *The Elementary Calendar*

Name _____

What Is Wrong with This Picture?

Circle the people who are NOT following the safety rules below.

Write the number of the broken rule next to the circle.

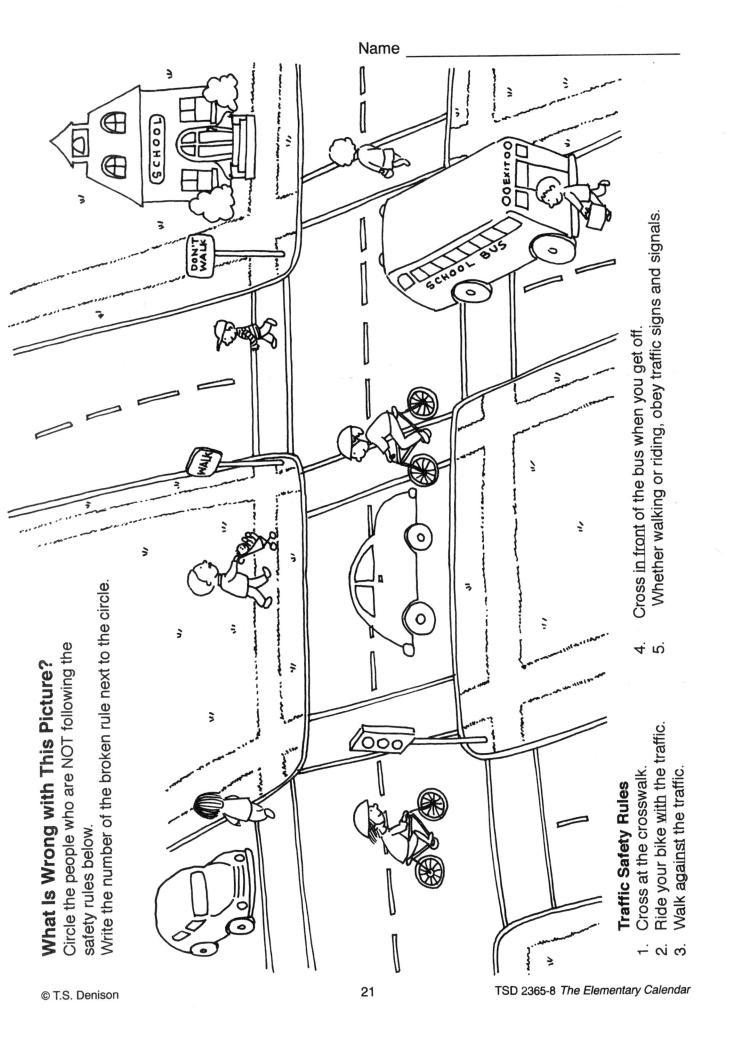

Traffic Safety Rules

1. Cross at the crosswalk.
2. Ride your bike with the traffic.
3. Walk against the traffic.
4. Cross in front of the bus when you get off.
5. Whether walking or riding, obey traffic signs and signals.

SEPTEMBER

SCHOOL

Please...

☐ Finish your work.
☐ Work neatly.
☐ Correct your work.
☐ Follow directions.

STAR STUDENT

_____ IS A _____

SUNSHINE CERTIFICATE

KOALA-TY WORK!

© T.S. Denison

TSD 2365-8 *The Elementary Calendar*

```
I  A  D  C  B  G  F  B  O  O  K  I  H  J
L  E  A  R  N  L  N  E  M  P  A  R  T  Q
N  I  R  P  E  N  C  I  L  S  V  T  U  E  X  Z
Y  B  A  C  D  F  E  H  L  U  N  C  H  A  G  J
I  R  E  A  D  I  N  G  K  M  L  N  O  C  P  B
Q  A  R  Z  S  M  V  U  W  X  G  L  Z  H  Y  U
A  R  C  B  D  U  F  E  G  I  Y  A  H  E  J  S
K  Y  L  N  C  S  E  P  T  E  M  B  E  R  M  P
L  P  Q  P  S  I  T  L  U  W  X  O  V  Z  A  B
C  E  D  A  F  C  L  A  S  S  G  R  H  J  I  K
L  N  M  P  O  Q  R  Y  C  T  V  D  U  W  V  X
   Y  Z  E  B  A  C  D  H  E  M  A  T  H  O
   H  W  R  I  T  E  G  O  K  J  Y  L  M  I
   N  P  O  R  Q  B  O  S  T  S  U  W
      I  V  X  Z  Y  L  B  A  E  D
```

Circle these words hidden in the apple.

BOOK	BELL	LEARN	ART
PENCIL	PAPER	PLAY	GYM
LIBRARY	WRITE	READING	LABOR DAY
LUNCH	CLASS	MATH	TEACHER
SCHOOL	BUS	MUSIC	SEPTEMBER

Name _____

Start

Start

CAN YOU CLIMB TO THE TOP?

Teacher: Fill the spaces from bottom to top with increasingly difficult math or language problems.

Back-to-School!

Write a back-to-school word on each apple. Color the apples and the basket and cut them out. Glue the apples and the basket to a piece of colored paper. Make sure the back-to-school words show. Put your name on the colored paper.

BACK TO SCHOOL

name _____

TSD 2365-8 *The Elementary Calendar*

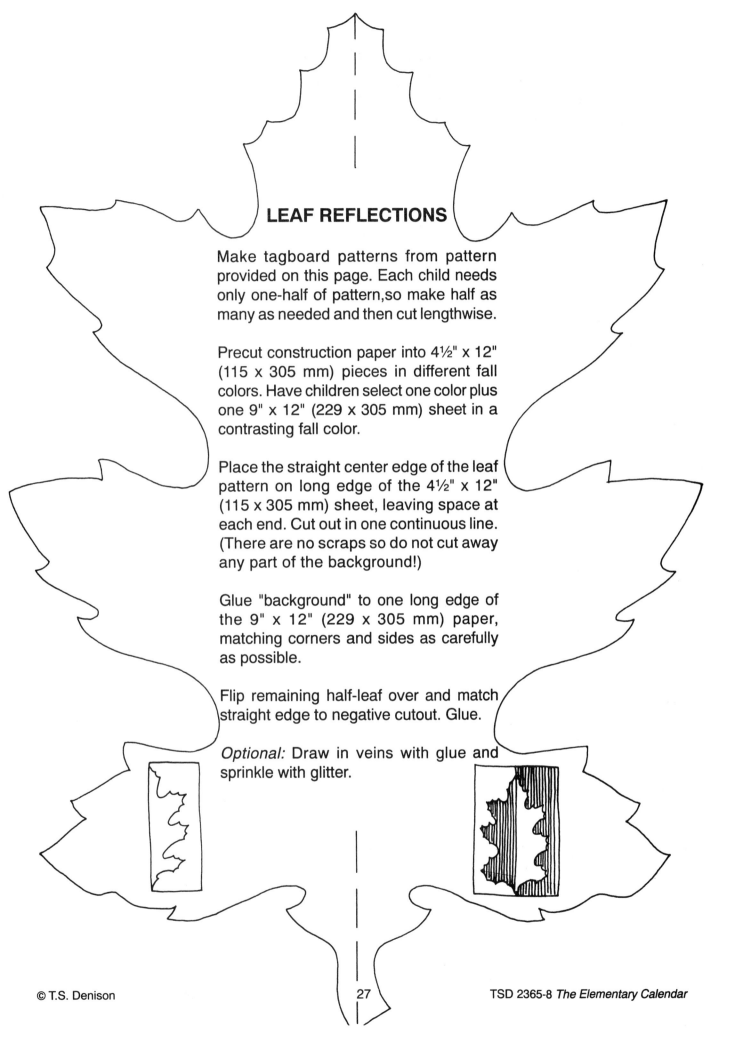

LEAF REFLECTIONS

Make tagboard patterns from pattern provided on this page. Each child needs only one-half of pattern, so make half as many as needed and then cut lengthwise.

Precut construction paper into 4½" x 12" (115 x 305 mm) pieces in different fall colors. Have children select one color plus one 9" x 12" (229 x 305 mm) sheet in a contrasting fall color.

Place the straight center edge of the leaf pattern on long edge of the 4½" x 12" (115 x 305 mm) sheet, leaving space at each end. Cut out in one continuous line. (There are no scraps so do not cut away any part of the background!)

Glue "background" to one long edge of the 9" x 12" (229 x 305 mm) paper, matching corners and sides as carefully as possible.

Flip remaining half-leaf over and match straight edge to negative cutout. Glue.

Optional: Draw in veins with glue and sprinkle with glitter.

Glue behind

September Patterns

October Contents

Sunday	Monday	Tuesday	Wednesday	Thursday	Friday	Saturday

TSD 2365-8 *The Elementary Calendar*

OCTOBER BIRTHDAYS

1	Jimmy Carter	39th president
2	Mahatma Gandhi	Indian leader; advocated nonviolent resistance
	Peanuts	Comic strip with Charlie Brown and Snoopy, introduced in 1950
4	Rutherford B. Hayes	19th president
	Damon Runyon	journalist and short story writer; *Guys and Dolls*
	Edward Stratemeyer	writer; *Nancy Drew*, *Tom Swift,* the *Hardy Boys*
5	Chester A. Arthur	21st president
11	Eleanor Roosevelt	worker for social causes; well-known first lady
13	Molly Pitcher	Mary Hays McCauley, Revolutionary War hero
	Margaret Thatcher	first woman prime minister of England
	The White House	cornerstone laid 1792
14	Dwight D. Eisenhower	World War II general; 34th president
	William Penn	founder of Pennsylvania; English quaker and reformer
	Peace Corps	established 1961
16	Noah Webster	lexicographer and writer
	Oscar Wilde	poet, playwright; *The Importance of Being Earnest*
17	Jupiter Hammon	America's first black poet, born 1711
20	John Dewey	philosopher, psychologist, educational reformer
23	Gertrude Ederle	first woman to swim the English Channel (in record time)
25	Admiral Richard E. Byrd	Antarctic explorer
	Pablo Picasso	leading painter of the 20th century
26	Statue of Liberty	1886 (gift from France in honor of 1876 centennial celebration)
27	Theodore Roosevelt	26th president
30	John Adams	2nd president
31	Juliet Gordon Low	founder of Girl Scouts of America

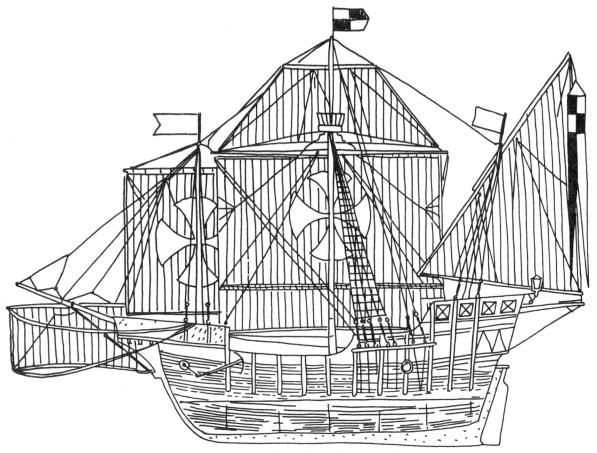

The *Santa Maria*

This is how Christopher Columbus's ship, the *Santa Maria*, really looked. The *Santa Maria* was only about eighty feet long and carried thirty-nine men. Columbus's other two ships, the *Niña* and *Pinta*, were even smaller! The *Pinta* carried twenty-six men and the *Niña* only twenty-two. Christopher Columbus and his crew crossed the Atlantic Ocean in these three tiny ships. No wonder the men were so afraid!

1. How many ships sailed to the New World? _____

2. The largest ship, the _____ was only _____ feet long.

3. The two smaller ships were called the _____ and the _____ .

4. Columbus and his crew crossed the _____ Ocean.

5. How many men sailed on the three ships altogether? _____

Activities
1. Make a picture of Columbus's three ships sailing across the ocean.
2. Measure eighty feet (about twenty-four meters) to see how long the *Santa Maria* was.
3. Write a story about how you might have felt if you had been one of the sailors on Columbus's voyage.
4. Find books and pictures about Christopher Columbus in your library. Show them to the class.
5. Use a globe to trace Columbus's voyage from Spain to the Bahamas.

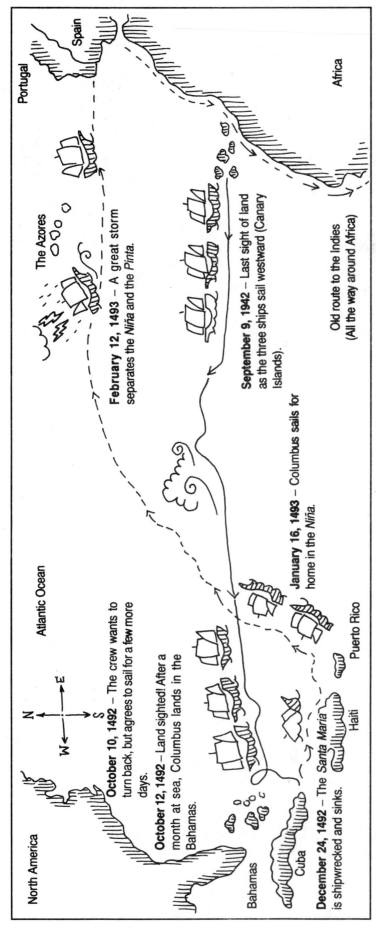

North America

Atlantic Ocean

N / E / S / W (compass)

October 10, 1492 – The crew wants to turn back, but agrees to sail for a few more days.

October 12, 1492 – Land sighted! After a month at sea, Columbus lands in the Bahamas.

Bahamas

Cuba

December 24, 1492 – The *Santa Maria* is shipwrecked and sinks.

Haiti

Puerto Rico

January 16, 1493 – Columbus sails for home in the *Niña*.

September 9, 1492 – Last sight of land as the three ships sail westward (Canary Islands).

Old route to the Indies (All the way around Africa)

The Azores

February 12, 1493 – A great storm separates the *Niña* and the *Pinta*.

Portugal

Spain

Africa

The Voyage of Christopher Columbus

Christopher Columbus was born in Genoa, Italy. He went to sea when he was nineteen years old. After several voyages, Columbus learned that the people of Portugal wanted to find a way to India, China, and Japan by sea so they could buy gold, jewels, and spices to bring home quickly.

Columbus believed that the world was round (not flat. He thought he could reach the rich lands of India, China, and Japan by sailing west around that world instead of going south around Africa and then heading east. The king of Portugal would not give Columbus all he wanted so Columbus went to Spain where Queen Isabella agreed to pay for his voyage. She gave him three ships: the *Niña*, the *Pinta*, and the larger *Santa Maria*. Columbus sailed west in August 1492.

Columbus and his crew sailed for over a month without seeing land. The men were afraid that they would never be able to get back home and they began to talk about taking over the ships. Finally, they agreed to sail for only two or three more days. Two days later, on October 12, 1492, land was seen and the tired crew landed in the "West Indies" because Columbus believed he had really reached India by sailing *west*. This is also why the Native Americans of North and South America were called Indians.

1 – red
2 – yellow
3 – blue
4 – green
5 – orange

6 – brown
7 – light blue
8 – black
0 – white

TSD 2365-8 *The Elementary Calendar*

School Lunch Week

Which are your two favorite school lunches?

1.

2.

Which are your least favorite lunches?

1.

2.

Why?

Do you usually bring your lunch from home or buy it at school?

bring _____   buy _____

What would you like the school to serve at lunchtime?
(Play fair! It has to be good for you and be low in price.)

Hot lunch:

Cold lunch:

Compare answers with those of your classmates.
Do you agree about anything? What?

What Shall We Make For Lunch?

vegetable soup	carrots	milk
chicken soup	lettuce	water
crackers	tomatoes	juice
	celery	

turkey	rye bread	apple
cheese	whole wheat bread	pear
tuna salad	hard roll	fruit cup
egg salad		ice cream
		brownie

Use the food list above to choose two healthy lunches.
Combine the foods and prepare them in any way you like.

❋ LUNCH ❋

_____

_____

_____

_____

_____

_____

❋ LUNCH ❋

_____

_____

_____

_____

_____

_____

4-H Club Week

The 4-H emblem is a green four-leaf clover with a white H on each leaflet to symbolize HEAD, HEART, HANDS, and HEALTH.

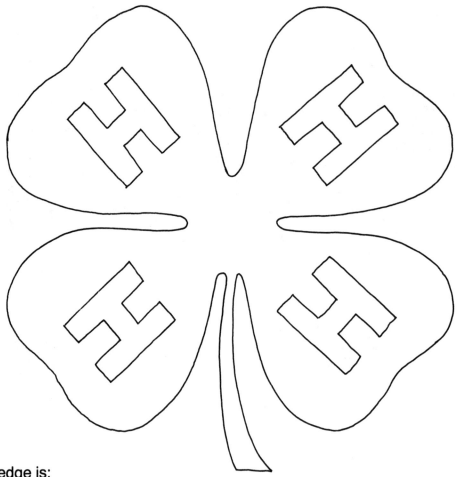

The 4-H pledge is:

I pledge my Head to clearer thinking,
my Heart to greater loyalty,
my Hands to larger service,
and my Health to better living,
for my club, my community,
my country, and my world.

The 4-H motto is: "To make the best better."

4-H Clubs are for boys and girls from nine to nineteen years of age and from all backgrounds and interests. (There are "Prep" Clubs for seven to nine year olds.) A group of five or more young people meet with an adult leader to work on many different projects such as gardening, woodworking, small animals, food and nutrition, karate, photography, etc. Members may also enjoy bicycling, consumer education, aerospace, and model rocketry. Completed projects can be submitted for judging and awards.

National Fire Protection Week

This house is a horror, haunted with hazards!
Find and circle the fire hazards in each room.
If you do not find ten, count again.

Trick or Treat Safety
by Edwina Witch

This costume is too long.
It will not do at all!
You know it will make you
Trip . . . and then fall!

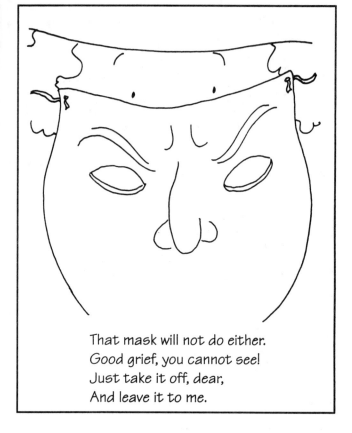

That mask will not do either.
Good grief, you cannot see!
Just take it off, dear,
And leave it to me.

Now try some of this GOOEY GREEN GLOP
(Until you turn green.)
It is just like a mask
If you see what I mean.

So you can see better,
Please take this bright light.
And please face the traffic.
Do not walk on the right.

And take someone with you
For safety you see.
Now whom do you choose?
Oh no dear! Not me!

All right, let us get going
(Trudge, trudge door to door.)
Just one more porch light.
(My feet are so sore!)

My dear, now you know
How to Halloween treat.
Just let me sit down
And get off these feet!

I am glad you enjoyed it,
My dear, so did I,
But next year, my dear . . .
Next year we shall fly!!!

Halloween Candy

Halloween candy,
Oh, so sweet.
Look what I got
For Trick or Treat!

Mom looked at it all
And said, "It's okay.
But you'd better not eat it
All in one day!"

Mom says, "Go easy!"
I guess that is best.
I'll eat just a little
And save all the rest.

My teeth will be happy
And so will my tummy,
But Halloween candy,
Oh boy! (And yum-yummy!)

Halloween "Treat" Ideas

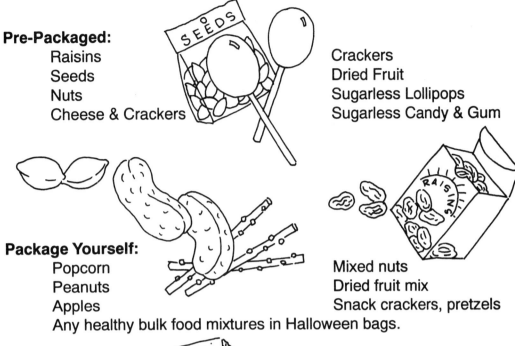

Pre-Packaged:
Raisins
Seeds
Nuts
Cheese & Crackers

Crackers
Dried Fruit
Sugarless Lollipops
Sugarless Candy & Gum

Package Yourself:
Popcorn
Peanuts
Apples
Any healthy bulk food mixtures in Halloween bags.

Mixed nuts
Dried fruit mix
Snack crackers, pretzels

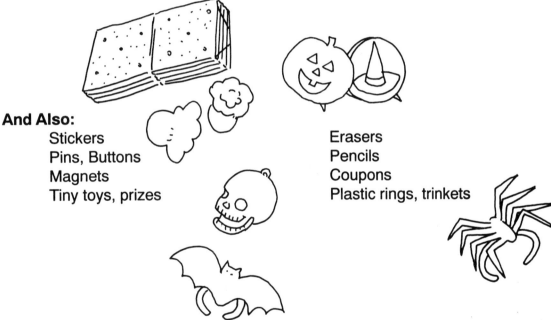

And Also:
Stickers
Pins, Buttons
Magnets
Tiny toys, prizes

Erasers
Pencils
Coupons
Plastic rings, trinkets

Use Your Imagination:
Try the supermarket, drugstore, five and dime, fabric center, school supply store, and other places for healthy snacks and nonfood "treats"!

Everyday Safety Rules for Halloween

Halloween is so exciting that sometimes we forget all about what we should (or should not) do to be safe. Halloween safety rules are the same rules we should already know and follow for safety every day of the year.

1. If you must walk in the road, walk on the left side facing the cars. Make sure drivers can see you.
2. If you must go out at night, carry a light and do not go alone.
3. Be very careful near people you do not know.
4. Make sure you can see and move safely. Do not wear anything that might make you trip or fall.
5. Be sure your parents know where you are and be home at the time they set.

Now Take This Halloween Safety Test and See How You Do!

Answer the following questions by checking YES or NO. Then write the number of the Everyday Safety Rule (above) that you should remember for each one.

On an ordinary day would I . . .   NO   YES   Rule #

1. wear clothes that might make me fall? _____ _____ _____

2. put something over my face so I could not see? _____ _____ _____

3. eat candy from a stranger without asking Mom or Dad? _____ _____ _____

4. walk on the wrong side of the road or run in the street? _____ _____ _____

5. go out after dark by myself? _____ _____ _____

6. go out after dark without a flashlight? _____ _____ _____

7. expect drivers to see me in the dark? _____ _____ _____

8. visit strange houses and people? _____ _____ _____

9. stay out late at night? _____ _____ _____

10. not tell my family where I was, or go where I was not supposed to go? _____ _____ _____

Name _____

Fill with math or language problems of increasing difficulty (or laminate and use mini-board games in which players must give correct answers.

OCTOBER

- ☐ I sat in my seat
- ☐ and kept my desk neat.
- ☐ I got my work done
- ☐ and had time for fun.
- ☐ I was very polite
- ☐ and did what was right.
- ☐ Raised my hand to speak
- ☐ . . . as a matter of fact . . .
- ☐ I was good all week!

Great Sailing

Student of the Week

Name _____

October Word Search

The words below are hidden across and down in the pumpkin.

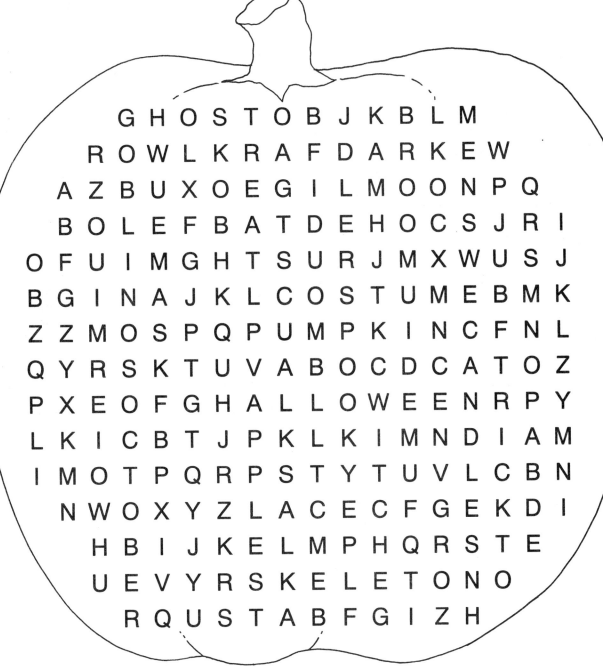

```
G H O S T O B J K B L M
R O W L K R A F D A R K E W
A Z B U X O E G I L M O O N P Q
B O L E F B A T D E H O C S J R I
O F U I M G H T S U R J M X W U S J
B G I N A J K L C O S T U M E B M K
Z Z M O S P Q P U M P K I N C F N L
Q Y R S K T U V A B O C D C A T O Z
P X E O F G H A L L O W E E N R P Y
L K I C B T J P K L K I M N D I A M
I M O T P Q R P S T Y T U V L C B N
N W O X Y Z L A C E C F G E K D I
H B I J K E L M P H Q R S T E
U E V Y R S K E L E T O N O
R Q U S T A B F G I Z H
```

Find and circle these words:

GOBLIN	TREAT	CAT	MASK
OWL	TRICK	MOON	CANDLE
GHOST	WITCH	APPLES	PUMPKIN
BAT	BROOM	SPOOKY	HALLOWEEN
COSTUME	DARK	OCTOBER	SKELETON

DIRECTIONS:

Extra fun: Have students complete problems and cut on dotted lines to open windows, then place over answer key you have made from an extra duplicate.

Haunted Halloween House

Color the Haunted Halloween House and cut it out. Cut on the dotted lines to open windows and doors. Color, cut out, and use the things below to "haunt" your house. Paste some things *behind* the windows for a surprise. Glue the finished house on a piece of black paper.

Use your **scraps** to make **more** spooky things for your **house.**

TSD 2365-8 *The Elementary Calendar*

Cut out the ghost (all the way around the spiral, too). Unscramble the Halloween words around the ghost and write them on the back. Add some words of your own or a Halloween story or joke.

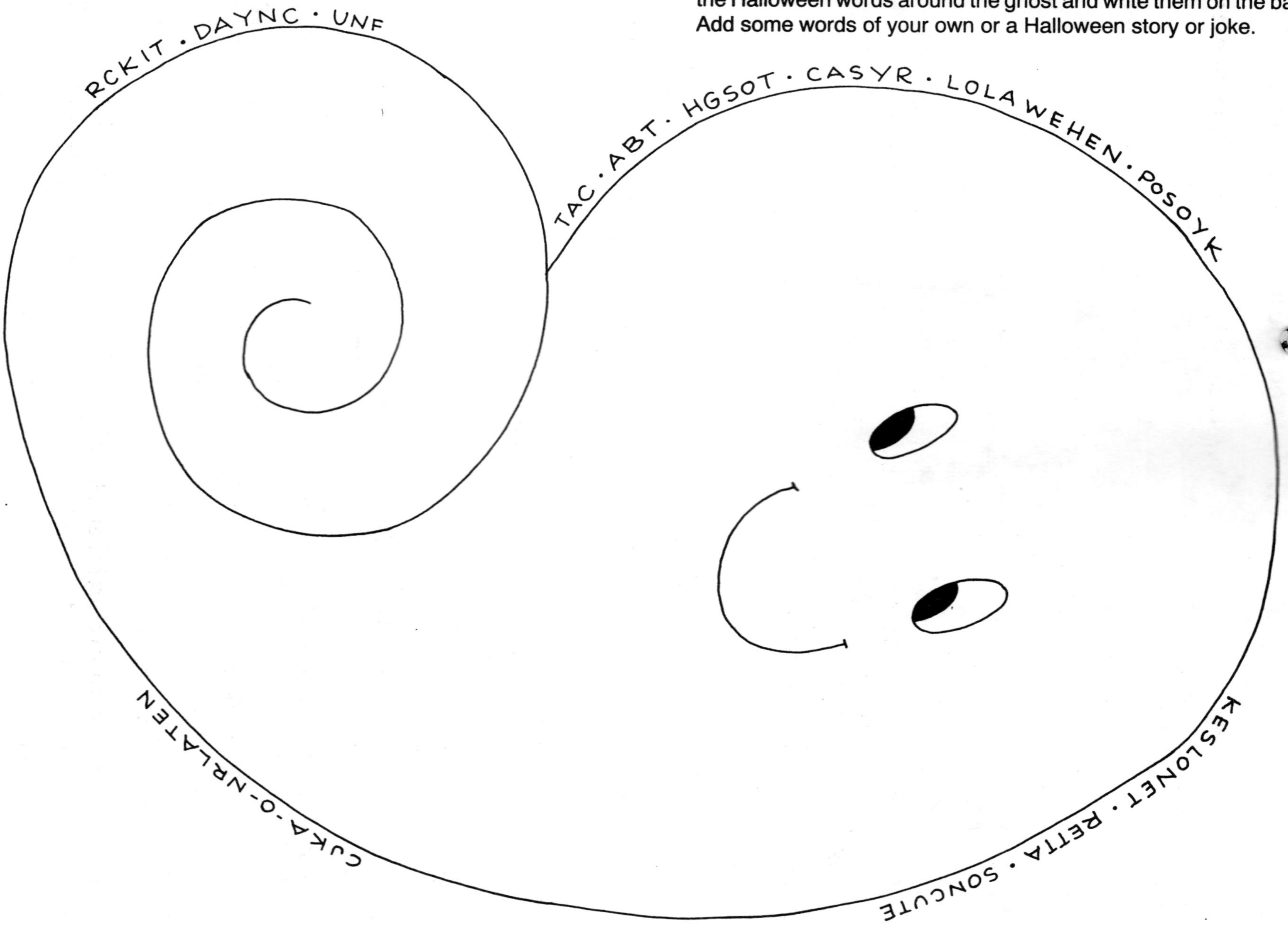

KESLONET · RETTA · SONCUTE

LOLA WEHEN · POSOYK

CASYR ·

TAC · ABT · HGSOT ·

RCKIT · DAYNC · UNF

CUKA-O-NRLATEN

Who Quilled the Wicked Witch?

Precut paper strips ½" (13 mm) wide in the following lengths (colors are only suggestions):

  12" (305 mm) hat (black), face (green), hair (white)
    6" (152 mm) nose (purple)
    5" (127 mm) eyes (orange)
    3" (76 mm) pupils (black)

Glue strips into rings to make face, eyes, and pupils. Glue pupils inside eyes.

Bring ends of nose strip together and glue (do not make ring). Glue eyes to each side of nose. Hold pieces together a few seconds, then glue inside the face ring and put aside to dry.

Fringe ends of hair strip and crinkle or curl.

Glue hair strip around top and sides of face ring.

Glue hat to either side of face as shown so that folded ends form brim.

Fold hat strip in half and fold up ends like "feet." Attach with glue.

Paper Strip Pumpkin with Bat

Precut: 12" x ½" (305 x 13 mm) orange strips, 1" x 3" (26 x 76 mm) black, 1" x 3" (26 x 76 mm) yellow construction paper

Use four orange strips to make two crosses, gluing them in the middle.

Glue one cross on top of the other, so that "spokes" are evenly spaced.

Bring up opposite "spoke" ends two at a time and glue, keeping them even.

Cut two corners from yellow rectangle for eyes and use the remainder for mouth. Glue.

Trace and cut out a bat from black paper. Glue inside the pumpkin or attach to end of a hanging string.

Attach string and hang, or use without string to decorate a party table.

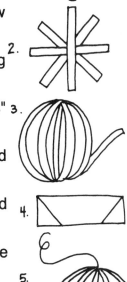

Spooky Spirals

Use pattern provided for small ghosts, or
have children copy the shape on large white paper.

Cut out the shape including spiral.
Add eyes and mouth with crayon or marker.

Staple on string and hang to twirl in the breeze

Halloween Houses
Have students cut narrow, uneven strips from black construction paper.

Glue strips to tracing or other paper to form a spooky house, cutting where needed and
leaving small spaces between strips. Discuss towers, roofs, porches, steps, columns, etc.

Weird Words
Choose Halloween words and draw them to show their meanings:
bat, web, spooky, mask, pumpkin, slimy, moon, etc.

or

Choose words as above and draw them with white crayon on white paper or
black crayon on black paper, pressing hard.

Wash over words with diluted tempera paint and a large brush.
Use black paint over white and white paint over black.
Words will appear since crayon resists paint.

October Patterns

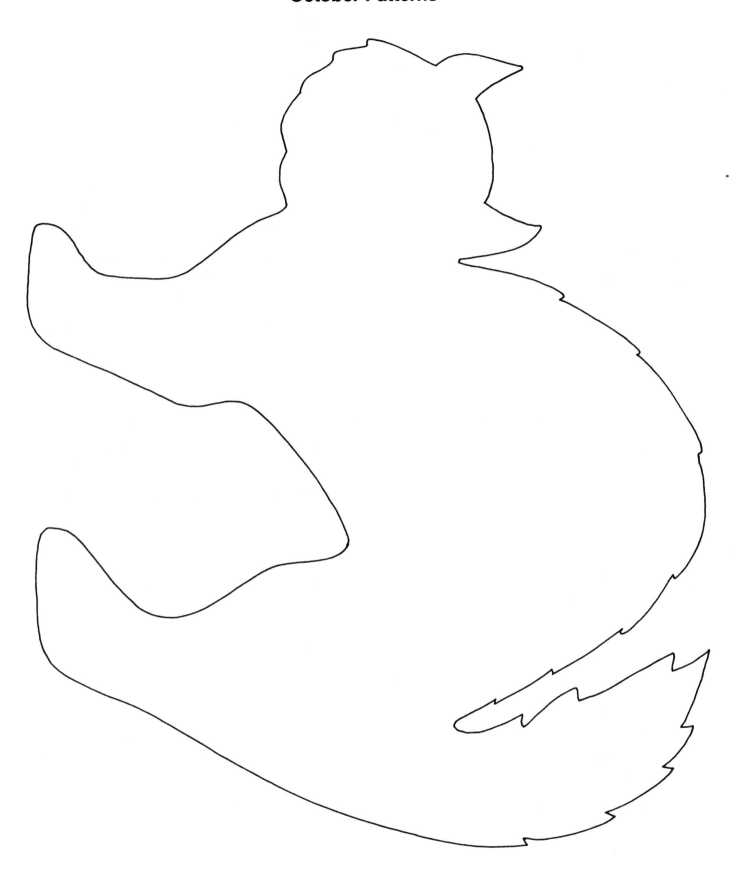

1 - orange
2 - yellow
3 - black
4 - green

5 - purple
6 - green
7 - brown
8 - light brown

TSD 2365-8 *The Elementary Calendar*

November Contents

Sunday	Monday	Tuesday	Wednesday	Thursday	Friday	Saturday

NOVEMBER BIRTHDAYS

2	Daniel Boone	frontiersman, explorer, folk hero
	Warren G. Harding	29th president
	James K. Polk	11th president
4	Will Rogers	writer, actor, humorist
6	John Philip Sousa	called America's "March King" composer
7	Marie Curie	Polish/French chemist; discovered use of radium in medicine; 1903 Nobel Prize for Physics and 1911 Nobel Prize for Chemistry
8	Edmund Halley	discovered & predicted return of comet named for him
11	George S. Patton	American general, World War II
	God Bless America	first performed on radio by Kate Smith, 1938
13	Robert Louis Stevenson	Scottish author; *Treasure Island* and *Kidnapped*
14	Robert Fulton	inventor who pioneered work in the development of the steamboat
15	Georgia O'Keefe	famous American avant-garde artist
16	W.C. Handy	William Christopher Handy, called the "Father of the Blues," composer, musician
18	Mickey Mouse	1928
19	James A. Garfield	20th president; assassinated in office
23	Franklin Pierce	14th president, not nominated for a second term
24	Zachary Taylor	12th president; died after one year in office
25	Andrew Carnegie	philanthropist; founded more than 2500 libraries
	Carry Amelia Nation	temperance leader
26	Mary Edwards Walker	early (b. 1832) women's rights leader; physician
29	Louisa May Alcott	American writer; *Little Women*
30	Sir Winston Churchill	British Prime Minister; World War II leader
	Mark Twain	writer Samuel Langhorne Clemens; *Tom Sawyer* and *Adventures of Huckleberry Finn*

Sandwich Day is November 3

Color and carefully cut out everything on the page. On another piece of paper, start with the bottom of the roll and make a sandwich! Overlap fillings a little as you build. Add the top of the roll for your finished sandwich.

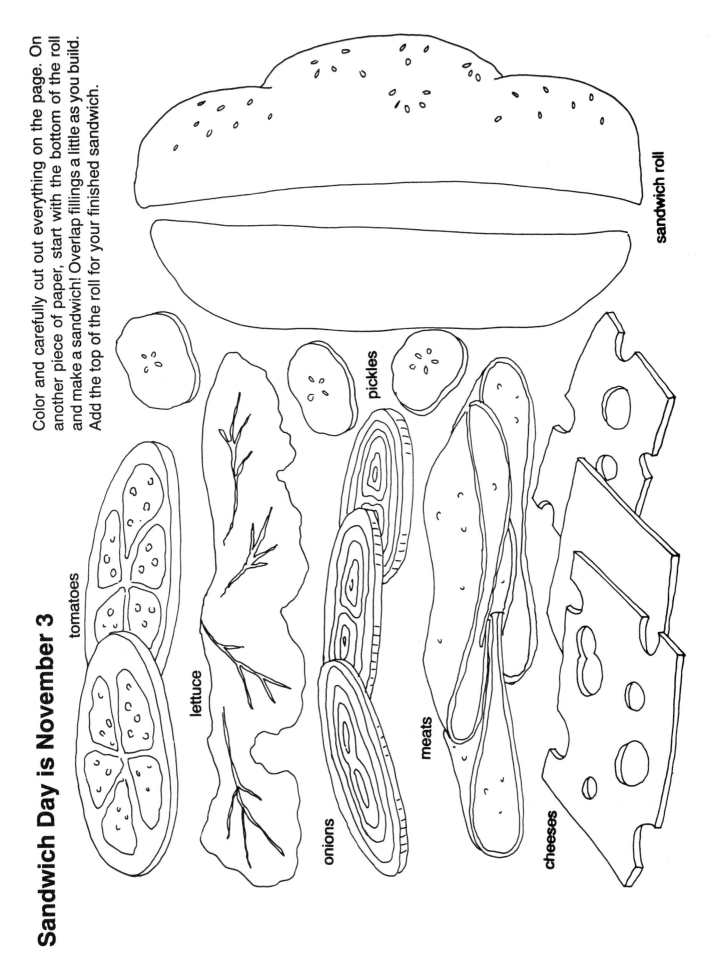

sandwich roll

tomatoes

lettuce

pickles

onions

meats

cheeses

Sandwich Day!

BOOK WEEK

Adler, David A.
Cam Jansen mysteries

Aliki
Overnight at Mary Bloom's

Allard, Harry
Miss Nelson Has a Field Day
Miss Nelson Is Back

Anglund, Joan Walsh
*Nibble, Nibble Mousekinz: A Tale of Hansel
and Gretel*

Bemelmans, Ludwig
Madeline stories

Bishop, Claire Huchet
The Five Chinese Brothers

Blume, Judy
Freckle Juice
*The One in the Middle Is the
Green Kangaroo*
The Pain and the Great One

Brandenberg, Franz
Aunt Nina and Her Nephews and Nieces
Aunt Nina's Visit
I Wish I Was Sick, Too!
Leo and Emily's Zoo

Brown, Marc
Arthur stories

Brown, Marcia, illustrated
Cinderella

Burton, Virginia Lee
The Little House
Mike Mulligan and His Steam Shovel

Cameron, Ann
Luanne Pig in the Talent Show
Luanne Pig in Witch Lady

Cleary, Beverly
Henry Huggins

Coombs, Patricia
Dorrie and the Halloween Plot
Dorrie and the Museum Case
Dorrie and the Witches' Camp

Cooney, Barbara
Chanticleer and the Fox

Eastman, P.D.
Are You My Mother?
Go, Dog. Go!
Sam and the Firefly

Flack, Marjorie
The Story About Ping
Wait for William

Gag, Wanda
Millions of Cats

Seuss, Dr.
The 500 Hats of Bartholomew Cubbins

Giff, Patricia Reilly
The Kids of the Polk Street School series

Gibbons, Gail
Dinosaurs
Trains
Fire! Fire!

Haywood, Carolyn
"B" Is for Betsy and other *Betsy and Eddie*
stories

Hoff, Syd
Danny and the Dinosaur
Sammy, the Seal
Julius

Keats, Ezra Jack
The Snowy Day

McCloskey, Robert
Make Way for Ducklings
Time of Wonder

Milhous, Katherine
  The Egg Tree

Minarik, Else Holmelund
  Little Bear

Moore, Clement C.
  The Night before Christmas

Mother Goose

Munari, Bruno
  Bruno Munari's *ABC*

Piper, Watty
  The Little Engine That Could

Potter, Beatrix
  The Tale of Peter Rabbit

Quackenbush, Robert
  Taxi to Intrigue and other *Miss Mallard* mysteries

Robbins, Ruth
  Baboushka and the Three Kings

Ross, Pat
  M and M mysteries

Sendak, Maurice
  Where the Wild Things Are

Sharmat, Marjorie Weinman
  I'm Terrific
  Nate the Great mysteries

Silverstein, Shel
  A Light in the Attic
  Where the Sidewalk Ends

Tressalt, Alvin
  White Snow, Bright Snow

Udry, Janice May
  A Tree Is Nice

Ward, Lynd
  The Biggest Bear

Yashima, Taro
  Crow Boy

Yolen, Jane
  Commander Toad and the Dis-asteroid
  Commander Toad in Space and other *Commander Toad* stories

I read: _____

By: _____

It was about: _____

_____

_____

_____

_____

_____

I especially liked:

_____

_____

_____

_____

This is a good book for:

_____

_____

_____

_____

Alexander B. Careful's

ABC Safety Tips

Alexander B. Careful's

ABC **Safety Tips**

"A _ _ _ _ _ _
be careful!"

says his mom

B _ _ _ _ _ _
your seatbelt.

Yes, that's right

C _ _ _ _ _
at the corner

. . . and watch the light!

D _ _ _ _
ride double.

Never! You hear?!

E _ _ _ _ _ day,
think safety.

Are you all right, dear?

F _ _ _ _ drill!

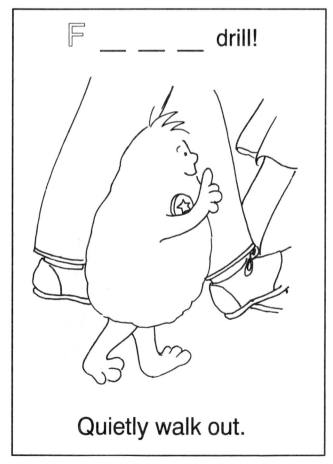

Quietly walk out.

G _
slowly on the stairs.

Alexander, watch out!

H _ _ _ _ _ _

are a must for bikers.

Your helmet looks just grand!

I _ _ streets?

Use extra care.

Then use a little sand.

J _ _ _ _

like this are not funny

as everybody knows.

K _ _ _ your knees

under your desk

and also all your toes.

L _ _ _ _ not
tied can make you fall.

Now then, tie that shoe!

M _ _ _ _ _ _ _
help with safety, too.

My dear, how nice of you!

N _ _ _ _ _
go near a strange dog.

Alexander! Get away!

O _ _ _
babies throw things

. . . but a ball is okay.

P _ _ _ ground
safety is important, too.

Alexander! Where are you?

Q _ _ _ _
during safety lessons

. . . and listen, too

R _ _ _ and obey
all traffic signs.

The rules are there for you!

S _ _ quietly
on the bus.

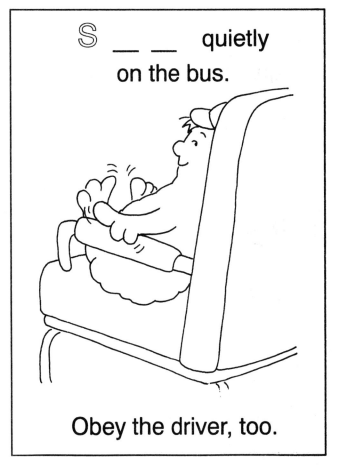

Obey the driver, too.

T __ __ __ turns
for safety.

That is always wise!

U __ __ two hands
on your bike

. . . and use your eyes!

V __ __ __ __ __
house? Stay away!

Alexander beware!

W __ __ __ in the
halls. Do not run!

Do not dare!

X- _ _ _ _
show broken bones.

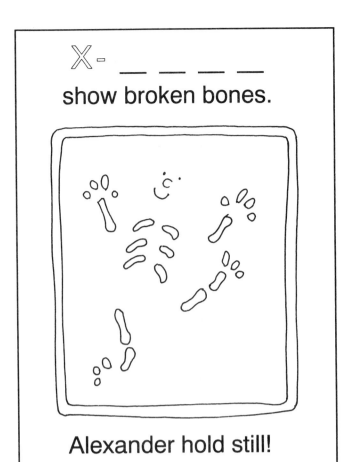

Alexander hold still!

Y _ _ can
keep yourself safe.

If only you will!

Z _ _ _
accidents, if you please.

Congratulations, Alexander.

Answer Key

Some words you will need:

always	never
buckle	only
cross	play(ground)
do not	quiet
every	read
fire (drill)	sit
go	take
helmets	use
icy	vacant
jokes	walk
keep	x-rays
laces	you
manners	zero

This award is just like Alexander's Extra Special Award for Being Careful. It was given to him by his grandfather, I.M. Careful. Alexander may only wear it when he remembers his safety lessons.

This award is for you!

THE
NATIVE
AMERICANS

Bird design by Acoma School child

TSD 2365-8 *The Elementary Calendar*

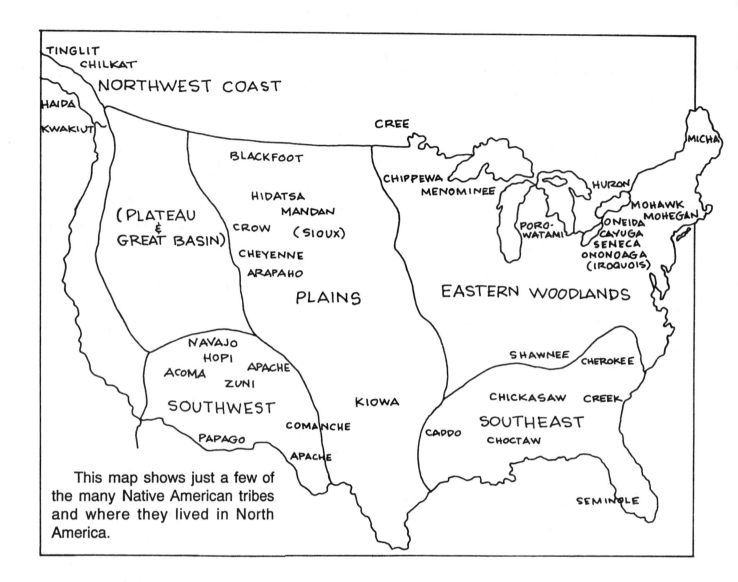

This map shows just a few of the many Native American tribes and where they lived in North America.

The word native means something that has always been in a place or belongs to a place. Native Americans lived in America long before the Europeans came (and before it was called America). They were called Indians because Christopher Columbus arrived in this New World believing he had reached India. Columbus called the people he saw Indians.

Early Native Americans made their living in different ways depending on where they lived. A Native American might be a hunter, a fisherman, a farmer, or a gatherer (of plants and other natural things he/she could use). Usually she/he was two or more of these things.

Native Americans who roamed the Plains were hunters. The buffalo they hunted gave them everything they needed to live: food, clothing, shelter, and tools. The northwest coast Native Americans were fishermen and hunters. In the Southwest, many Native Americans were peaceful farmers living in pueblo villages and enjoying the warm climate. Others made a living by hunting and by raiding what they needed from different tribes. In the eastern woodlands and the Southeast, Native Americans could fish, hunt, gather food, and even raise crops in the fertile soil.

The Native American people had deep feelings about nature; about the earth, sky, and waters; the plants and animals; the sun and moon; the weather and the seasons of the year. They loved, respected, and celebrated these natural things that were such an important part of their lives. Native Americans used materials from nature to make what they needed and to decorate what they had. Art was not made to hang on a wall or to put on display. Art and nature were a part of everyday life.

From clay and grasses, the Native American made pottery and baskets to carry and store things. From cotton fibers and animal hair and skins, she/he made clothing and shelter. From bone, wood, and stone she/he made tools and weapons. Bones, shells, fur, claws, teeth, feathers, and porcupine quills decorated all of these things. When European explorers and settlers came, Native Americans incorporated the things brought to the "New World" into their own way of life. Metal tools made wood carving easier; Spanish sheep gave fine wool for blankets; Spanish silver made beautiful jewelry; tiny beads from Europe decorated clothing and many other objects.

Many arts and crafts were lost when Native Americans were driven off their lands and onto reservations in the west. Some Native American artists and a few friends worked to save some of the beautiful art. Today, Navajo rugs and jewelry, Pueblo jewelry, Hopi pottery, and the woodcarvings of the Northwest are famous over the world.

TSD 2365-8 *The Elementary Calendar*

Hopi

Navajo, Apache, Hopi, Zuni, Acoma, Laguna, Pima, Papago, Mojave

The tribes of the southwest learned many things from the Mexican Indians and from the Spanish who built colonies in this "New Spain." They learned silver-working and made beautiful silver and turquoise jewelry. They made hand-shaped pottery with wonderful red, black, and white designs, and they wove baskets in many different patterns. To heal the sick, they made sand paintings and called upon helpful spirits called *kachinas*.

The Hopi believed that *kachinas* once lived among human beings and helped them in many ways. There were *kachinas* for animals, flowers, the sun, moon, stars, and many other things—250 in all. *Kachina* costumes were worn for dances and ceremonies. *Kachina* dolls were given to children for good luck and protection.

For these peaceful farmers every person was important to the tribe; no one person was better than another. The Hopi tribe as a whole was most important. They did not fight the Spanish or other settlers. The Hopi kept their customs secret and pretended to accept European ways so that their people would be left alone. Because they did not fight, and because the white man did not want the difficult land of the Southwest, the Hopi were left in peace and were able to keep their customs and traditions intact.

Today, Hopi pottery, baskets, sand paintings (now glued to wood), silver jewelry, and *kachina* dolls are sold to tourists and collectors. These crafts are admired throughout the world.

SOUTHWEST

Not all of the southwestern tribes were peaceful farmers. The Navajo and Apache were raiders who did some hunting, but generally took what they needed during raids on the peaceful Pueblo tribes and the European settlers. The Navajo and Apache became fierce enemies of the Spanish Mexicans who entered their territory.

In 1863, after the United States had bought the Southwest from Spain, the government decided to oust the Navajo and Apache from their land. Kit Carson was sent to round them up and move the Native Americans out of the area. After five years away from their home, the Navajo promised to live in "perpetual peace" with the whites and with other Native American neighbors. They were allowed to return to a part of their former lands and live on a reservation.

The Navajo incorporated materials from other cultures into their own art and craft work. They began making jewelry from U.S. silver dollars and Mexican pesos. Pueblo wives, stolen in raids, taught the Navajo how to weave; Spanish merino sheep gave fine wool. Later, English woolens were unraveled for their beautiful red yarn and the Navajo began selling their famous red, black, and white blankets and rugs to tourists. Navajo silverwork and handsome rugs are popular everywhere today.

Only the Apache refused to surrender to the white man. They kept to themselves and continued raiding and fighting fiercely until their leader, Geronimo, was forced to surrender to the United States army in 1868.

Apache

Creek, Choctaw, Chickasaw, Cherokee, Seminole

Tribes of the Southeast were farmers. They grew pumpkins, squash, beans, colored corn, and gourds. Their farms were laid out around a small village with an open area in the middle. This open space was called a "stomp ground" and was used for dances and for ceremonies.

In winter, homes were made of poles woven with smaller branches and covered with mud to keep out the cold. In summer, the houses were open on the sides under long roofs covered with palmetto. Platforms along the walls inside were used for sleeping. The Florida Seminoles called these open houses *chickees*.

Clothing of the southeast tribes was made from deerskin. The skins were also used for trade. In colonial times, thousands and thousands of skins were traded to the Europeans.

The white man came to the Southeast very early and began to settle there. The tribes traded with all of them, the Spanish, the French, and the English. They watched Europeans struggle to control the "new" land. The Cherokee, the largest southeastern tribe, sided with the English during the Revolutionary War and then with the Americans in the War of 1812.

By the early 1800s, the Native Americans of the Southeast had begun to adopt the ways of the European settlers. They adopted plow agriculture, animal husbandry, owned slaves, developed laws and written language, and sent their children to school. The Creek, Choctaw, Chickasaw, Cherokee, and Seminole were called "the five civilized tribes" because they assimilated the culture of the European settlers.

Seminole

*Beaded Design
(Creek)*

Being "civilized" did not help these tribes when the settlers wanted more of the tribes' land to grow even more cotton. President Andrew Jackson ordered the tribes rounded up and herded west to land across the Mississippi. Many people died of starvation, cold, and sickness on the long march. Today we call this forced march "The Trail of Tears."

Only the Seminoles, who had moved to Florida, fought against the American soldiers. The American soldiers were especially angry because the Seminoles hid black slaves who ran away from southern plantations. The Seminoles were driven into the Florida swamps where they fought for seven years. They killed 1500 white soldiers, but at the end of the war, there were only 500 Seminoles left. Those few hid deep in the Everglades— on land the white man did not want.

Today, the Seminoles and their neighbors the Miccosukee still live in the Everglades. Many run small "trading posts" where they put on alligator shows and sell souvenirs to visiting tourists.

Silk Design (Cherokee)

TSD 2365-8 *The Elementary Calendar*

Sioux

Blackfoot

THE PLAINS

Beaded Baby Carrier (Kiowa)

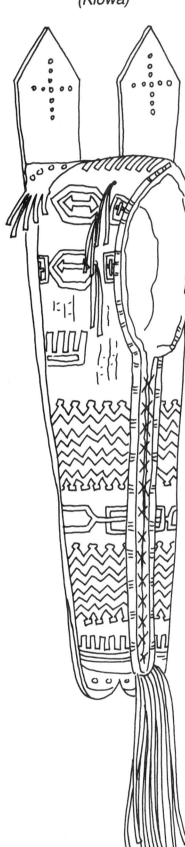

Sioux , Sihasapa (Blackfoot), Mandan, Cheyenne, Arapaho, Shoshone, Kiowa, Piegan, Crow, Hidatsa

When we think of the "Wild West" or "cowboys and Indians," it is the Plains warrior we see in our imagination. He wears a feathered war bonnet and rides a fast and beautiful horse. He lives in a pointed teepee and carries a rifle in his raids against the white man.

The Plains tribes were buffalo hunters. The buffalo gave them everything they needed: hides and hair for clothing and shelter, meat for food, and bones for tools and other items. Their lives depended upon following and hunting the great herds.

Until the Spanish brought the horse, the Plains tribes kept dogs to help move their camps from place to place. When they saw the first horses they called them "big dogs." The horse and the European rifle made life much easier for the Plains Indians. They could follow and kill the buffalo, move goods over the prairie, and raid other tribes much more easily.

Because the Plains tribes had to carry all their belongings with them, their art was mostly the decoration of hides, clothing, and everyday objects. Porcupine quills and the European "trade beads" decorated war shirts, gun cases, moccasins, and many other things. Sometimes teepees and hides were painted to show a warrior's adventures.

When white settlers began to move west, soldiers killed thousands of buffalo in order to drive the Native Americans off the plains. Although the tribes tried to fight back, they did not understand the white man's idea of war (killing off an entire tribe instead of gaining honor by stealing a few horses) until it was too late. There were too many white men with too many guns and the Plains warriors, weakened by diseases and alcohol brought by the white man, were herded onto reservations.

Legging Moccasins (Cheyenne)

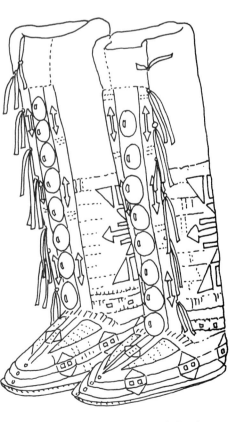

NORTHWEST COAST

Haida, Tlingit, Chilkat, Kwakiutl

The riches of the water, land, forests, and a good climate made life easy for Native Americans of the northwest coast. They fished for salmon and hunted land and sea animals. They used the strong cedar wood of the forest and European metal tools to build large "apartment" homes, to make dugout canoes, and to carve huge totem poles.

These northwest tribes were very rich. The chief and his family were royalty; wealthy relatives, warriors, and artists were next in rank. There was a large group of common people and then there were slaves to do the hard chores.

In the winter the tribes held ceremonies with dances, masks, and fancy costumes. The Kwakiutl *Potlatch* was a huge party given to celebrate a royal wedding, a new baby, or to introduce a young man of the wealthy class. It was a party that showed off the wealth of the chief. Many rich gifts were given to guests. Since the visiting tribe had to give an even fancier party, the *Potlatch* became a contest to see which was the most powerful and richest tribe.

The northwestern tribes are most famous for their wood carvings and colorful blankets which show the spirits of the animals that were so important to them—the bear, beaver, whale, and other animals of the area.

Chilkat

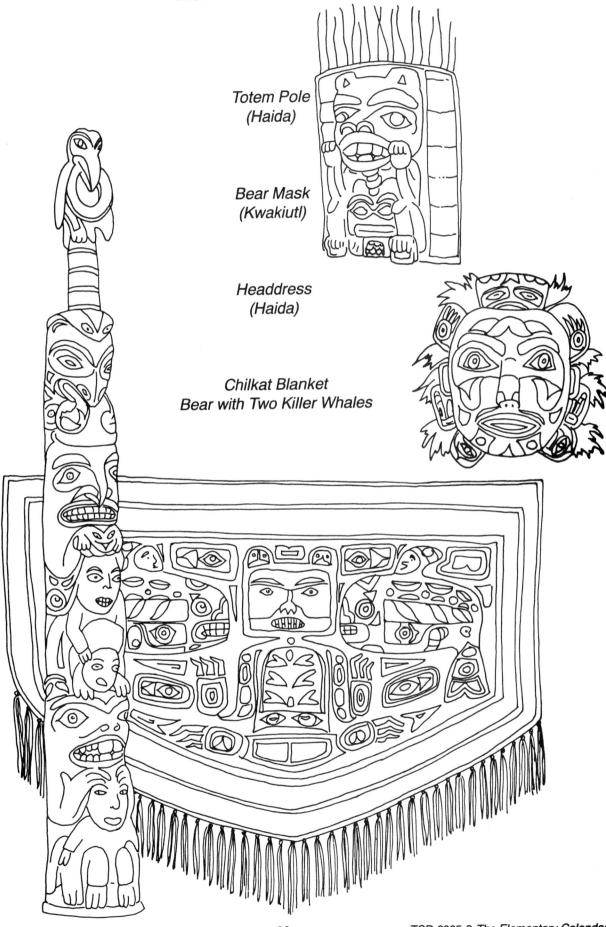

Totem Pole
(Haida)

Bear Mask
(Kwakiutl)

Headdress
(Haida)

Chilkat Blanket
Bear with Two Killer Whales

Iroquois Longhouse

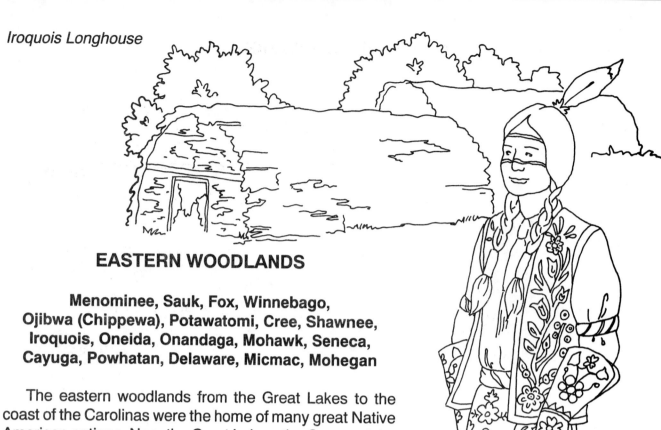

EASTERN WOODLANDS

Menominee, Sauk, Fox, Winnebago, Ojibwa (Chippewa), Potawatomi, Cree, Shawnee, Iroquois, Oneida, Onandaga, Mohawk, Seneca, Cayuga, Powhatan, Delaware, Micmac, Mohegan

The eastern woodlands from the Great Lakes to the coast of the Carolinas were the home of many great Native American nations. Near the Great Lakes, the Cree and the Ojibwa (Chippewa) drove out many other tribes to take over the rich fur trade with the white man. The mighty Iroquois nation—the Oneida, Onandaga, Mohawk, Seneca, Cayuga and Tuscarora—settled in New York State.

These tribes had many different life styles. Some, like the Ojibwa, lived in wigwams and roamed large areas, hunting and trapping for the fur trade. Others, like the Iroquois, lived in villages of "longhouses" and were farmers as well as hunters and gatherers. They taught the first white settlers how to raise corn, beans, and squash.

With good soil for farming, plenty of fish from the lakes and rivers, and many kinds of game from the forests, life was not hard for the woodlands tribes. They had time for dances and ceremonies, and for making pottery and beautifully decorated clothing. Moose and deerskins were softened and decorated with moosehair and porcupine quills. After the white man came, the tribes traded for velvets, silk thread, and tiny beads. They copied European floral motifs and used the designs to decorate hides, clothing, bags, and moccasins with the silks and tiny beads.

As the white man claimed more and more land, these tribes were rounded up by the American government and forced to move westward across the Mississippi, and finally, onto reservations.

Chippewa (Ojibwa)

EASTERN WOODLANDS

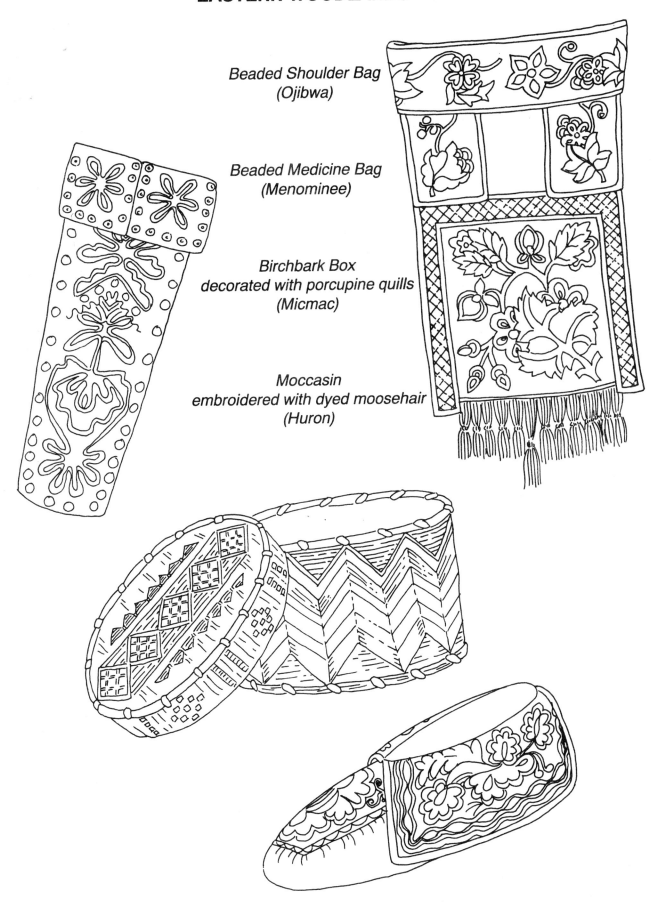

Beaded Shoulder Bag
(Ojibwa)

Beaded Medicine Bag
(Menominee)

Birchbark Box
decorated with porcupine quills
(Micmac)

Moccasin
embroidered with dyed moosehair
(Huron)

TSD 2365-8 *The Elementary Calendar*

THE SOUTHWEST

Sun Kachina
(Hopi sand painting)

Follow the numbers
to color the Sun Kachina.

> 1 – red
> 2 – yellow
> 3 – turquoise
> 4 – green
> 5 – blue
> 6 – light brown
> 7 – black

The Hopi believed *kachinas* were spirits sent to earth to help them in many ways. They dressed in *kachina* costumes for ceremonial dances and gave *kachina* dolls to children. There were 250 Hopi *kachinas*.

Many Southwest tribes used colored sand to make paintings, like this one, that asked the *kachinas* for help. This Sun Kachina was to help bring the sun to the crops for a good harvest.

Bear Mask

Use the numbers to color the left side of this Kwakiutl bear mask. Then color the right side to match.

1 – red	2 – blue	3 – yellow	4 – green	5 – light brown	7 – black

The Northwest Coast tribes lived along the water from Washington to Alaska. Their carved wooden totem poles and masks are famous today. They also wove beautiful and colorful blankets to keep warm. They fished and hunted for food.

Name _____

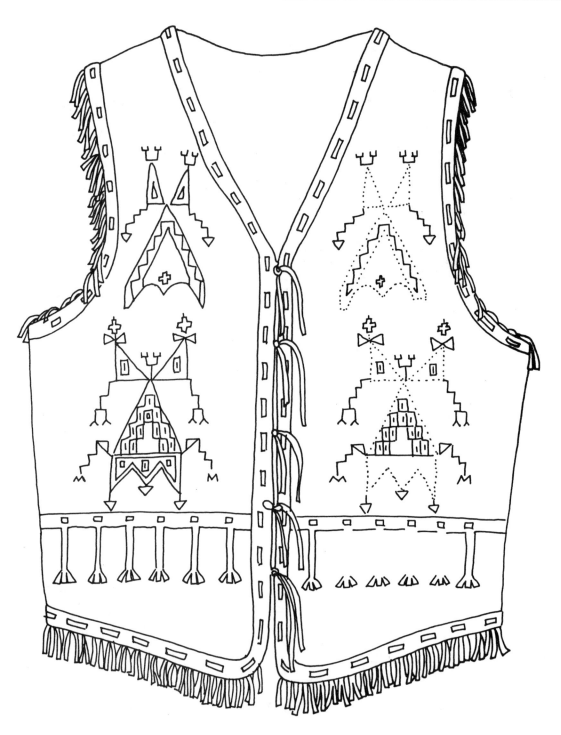

Sioux Vest

This Sioux vest is covered with tiny beads. Look at the design on the left to help you finish the design on the right. (The dots will help, too.) Then color the picture.

The Sioux tribes lived on the plains. They rode horses and moved their camps frequently to follow and hunt the buffalo. The buffalo gave the plains tribes everything they needed: hides for teepees and clothing, meat for food, and bones for tools.

EASTERN WOODLANDS

Name _____

Potawatomi Bead Design

These shapes were left out of the Potawatomi bead design above. Look at the design and use a pencil to draw in the missing parts.

The Potawatomi tribe lived near the Great Lakes where Michigan is today. They sold furs to the traders. Woodland tribes such as the Potawatomi borrowed European floral designs like these and sewed them into beautiful beadwork patterns of their own.

HUNTING TRIBES WORD SEARCH

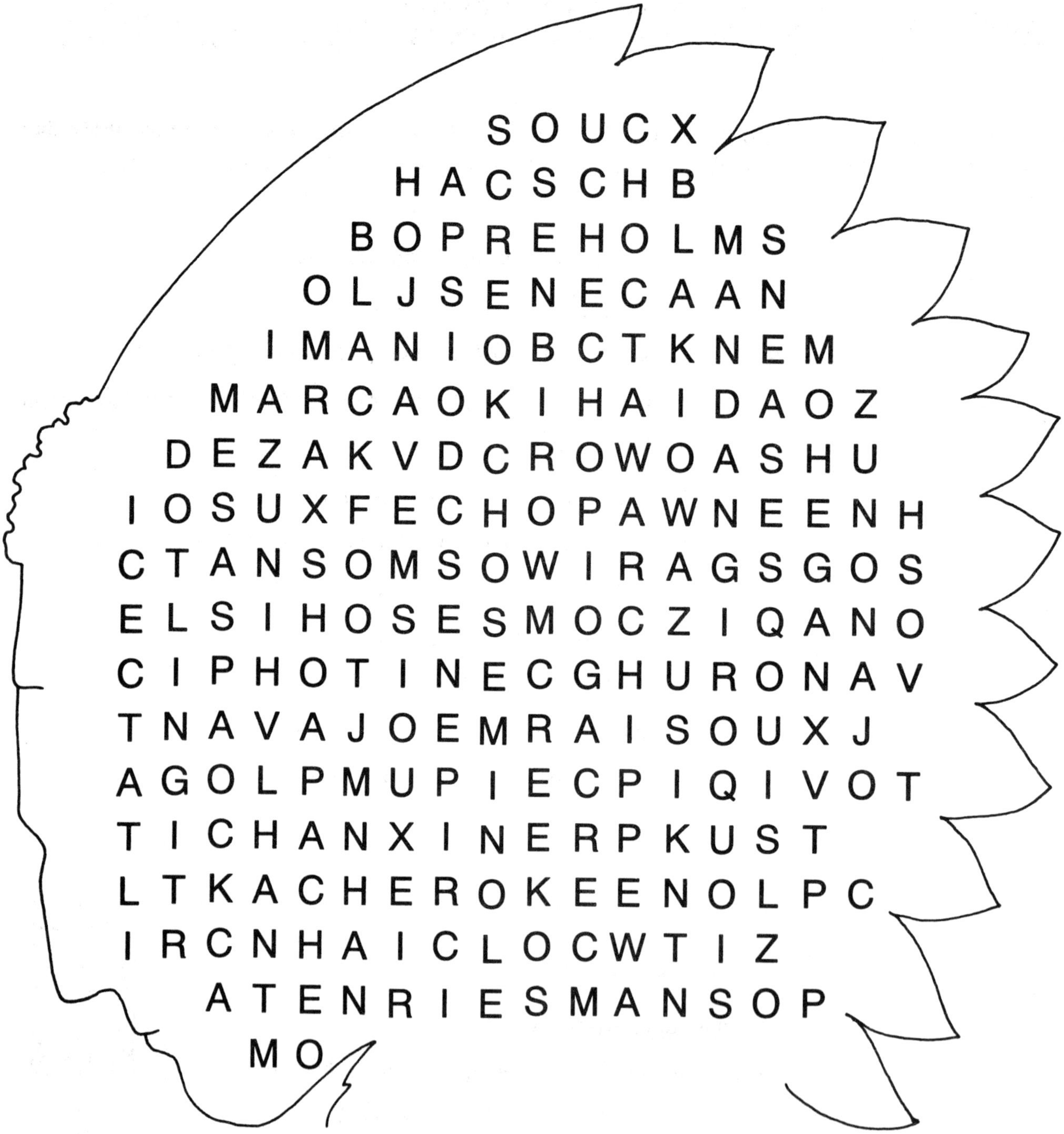

```
        S O U C X
      H A C S C H B
    B O P R E H O L M S
    O L J S E N E C A A N
    I M A N I O B C T K N E M
  M A R C A O K I H A I D A O Z
  D E Z A K V D C R O W O A S H U
I O S U X F E C H O P A W N E E N H
C T A N S O M S O W I R A G S G O S
E L S I H O S E S M O C Z I Q A N O
C I P H O T I N E C G H U R O N A V
T N A V A J O E M R A I S O U X J
A G O L P M U P I E C P I Q I V O T
T I C H A N X I N E R P K U S T
L T K A C H E R O K E E N O L P C
I R C N H A I C L O C W T I Z
  A T E N R I E S M A N S O P
    M O
```

Find and circle the names of these tribes in the puzzle.
(Watch out for spelling! This puzzle is tricky!

HAIDA	APACHE	HURON	MOHEGAN
TLINGIT	SIOUX	PAWNEE	CHOCTAW
HOPI	MANDAN	CHIPPEWA	CHEROKEE
ZUNI	BLACKFOOT	SENECA	SEMINOLE
NAVAJO	CROW	IROQUOIS	CREEK

Name _____

Please State Your Name
(And Name Your State)

The names of many of our states were borrowed from Native American words. Look at the lists below. Find the Native American name for the state and write its letter on the line next to that state.

_____ Alabama

_____ Alaska

_____ Arkansas

_____ Illinois

_____ Iowa

_____ Minnesota

_____ Nebraska

_____ North/South Dakota

_____ Tennessee

_____ Utah

_____ Texas

_____ Mississippi

a. *Yuuttaa*, Ute name for themselves

b. *Tanasi*, "river" in Cherokee

c. name means "father of waters" in Algonquian

d. *Alakhskhakh*, Aleut word meaning "land that is not an island"

e. *Tihsis*, Caddo place name

f. *Dakhota*, "the friendly ones" in Sioux

g. *Akansea*, Quapaw word meaning "downstream people"

h. *Alibamu*, a Muskogean tribe

i. *Illiniuek*, "men" in Algonquian

j. *Ayuba*, Dakota for "sleepy"

k. *Minisota*, Sioux for "clouded water" (river)

l. *Nibdhathka*, Omaha for "flat river"

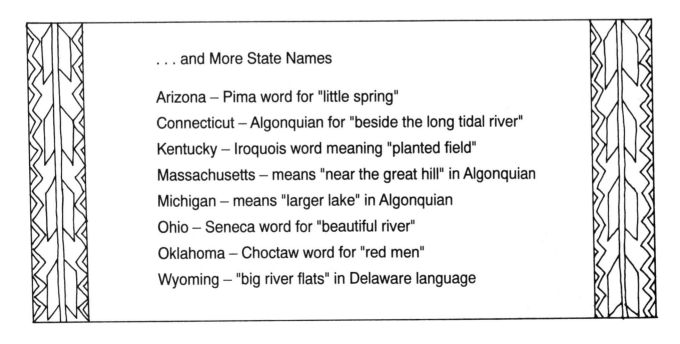

. . . and More State Names

Arizona – Pima word for "little spring"

Connecticut – Algonquian for "beside the long tidal river"

Kentucky – Iroquois word meaning "planted field"

Massachusetts – means "near the great hill" in Algonquian

Michigan – means "larger lake" in Algonquian

Ohio – Seneca word for "beautiful river"

Oklahoma – Choctaw word for "red men"

Wyoming – "big river flats" in Delaware language

You have
"Tur-'Key" to Success!

HAS LEARNED
ALL OF OUR

NOVEMBER
GOOD NEWS!

for _____
from _____

Works and plays well
with others.

Is an excellent worker.

Follows directions well.

Completes work promptly.

Handles materials carefully.

Is very dependable.

Certificate of Thanks
Awarded to

for

Thanksgiving Word Search

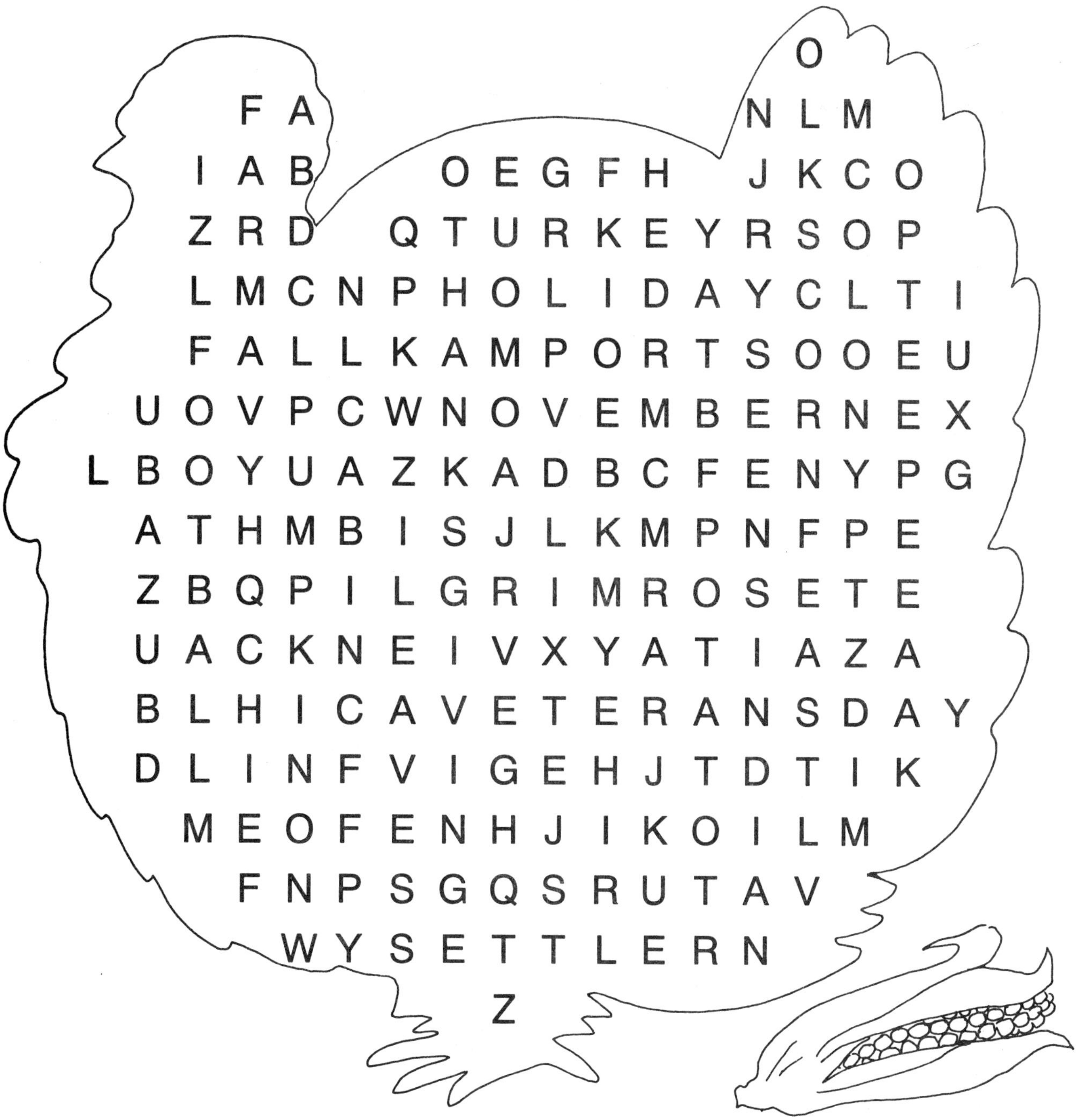

```
          O
        N L M
F A   O E G F H  J K C O
I A B Q T U R K E Y R S O P
Z R D   P H O L I D A Y C L T I
L M C N P H O L I D A Y C L T I
F A L L K A M P O R T S O O E U
U O V P C W N O V E M B E R N E X
L B O Y U A Z K A D B C F E N Y P G
A T H M B I S J L K M P N F P E
Z B Q P I L G R I M R O S E T E
U A C K N E I V X Y A T I A Z A
B L H I C A V E T E R A N S D A Y
D L I N F V I G E H J T D T I K
M E O F E N H J I K O I L M
F N P S G Q S R U T A V
W Y S E T T L E R N
        Z
```

Find and circle these words:

TURKEY	COLONY	POTATO	HOLIDAY
FEAST	SETTLER	TEEPEE	PUMPKIN
PILGRIM	CABIN	CHIEF	NOVEMBER
INDIAN	FARM	LEAVES	VETERAN'S DAY
FALL	CORN	FOOTBALL	THANKSGIVING

Colonial Days
Word Search

Name _____

```
                              I P
    Z K S E A P O R T A C S L
    L U C I M H T E E P E E P A
    P M O N A I W J K C A B I N
    I O L D Y J N P N O M A N T
    J L U O E F T E E P N E I N A I
    K G N N P L C D H W S R X I T L
    M R T Y E O N L F U T I A N I U
    I A B N W C H A L I C U G O
    M I N D E P U R I T A N T N
    S N E E R F G M H U J I W K
    Z D U N I T E D S T A T E S
    N O Q C N R V X K I L F A Z
    E G J E D C B G H O K M V L
    W A S H I N G T O N P S I T
    X Y U D A F R I V E R A N W
    N T H A N K S G I V I N G F
```

Find and circle these words:

CABIN	INDIAN	AMERICA	THANKSGIVING
SEAPORT	TEEPEE	MOUNTAIN	CONSTITUTION
PILGRIMS	RIVER	MAYFLOWER	INDEPENDENCE
PURITAN	FARM	PLANTATION	UNITED STATES
SPINNING	WEAVING	COLONY	WASHINGTON

TSD 2365-8 *The Elementary Calendar*

NATIVE AMERICAN BOOKMARKS & HEADBANDS

To make a bookmark:
Color the bookmark on the right. Use a lot of red, yellow, blue, and a little black.

Use geometric shapes to make your own Native American designs on the other bookmark. Color it as well.

Cut out the bookmarks and fringe the ends with scissors.

To make a headband:
Cut out your bookmark and the one on the right. (Match the designs if you like.) Do not fringe. Overlap an end of each and glue or paste. Try it on. Overlap the other two ends and glue together to fit your head.

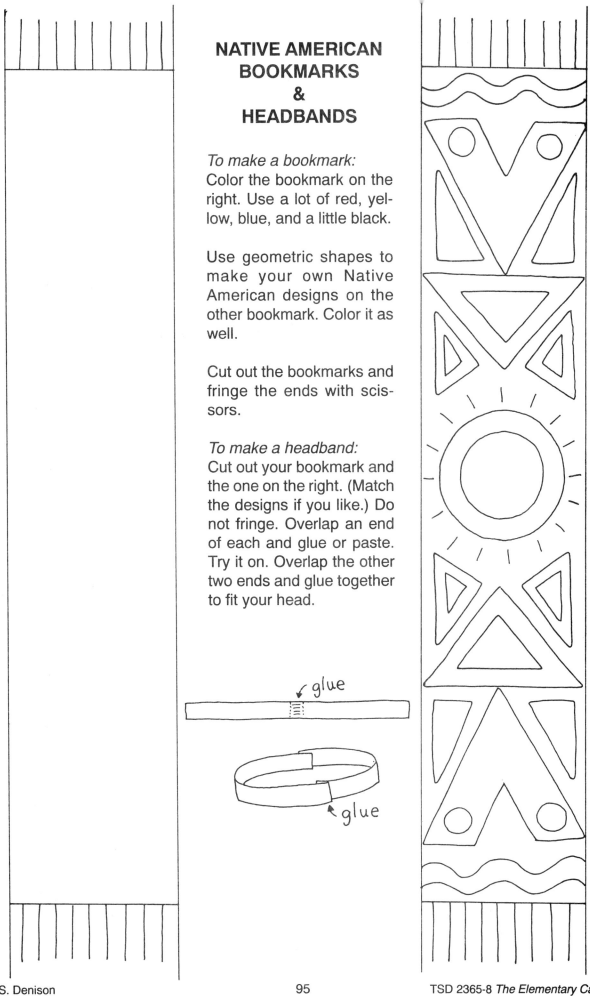

glue

glue

TSD 2365-8 *The Elementary Calendar*

TURKEY AND PILGRIM HAT

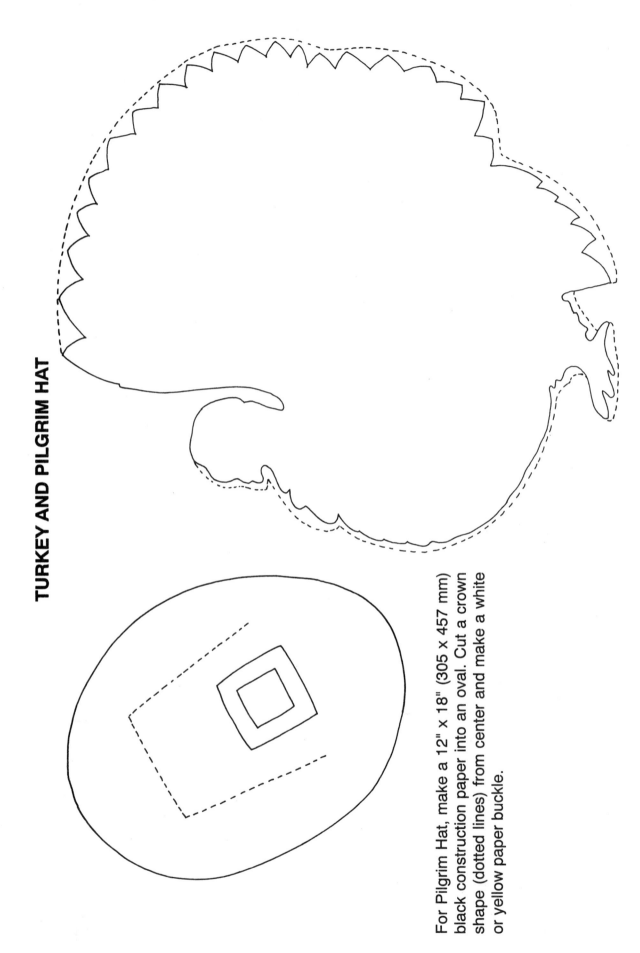

• To simplify turkey, cut tail and wing with pinking shears.
• For younger children, use dotted lines to make pattern.

For Pilgrim Hat, make a 12" x 18" (305 x 457 mm) black construction paper into an oval. Cut a crown shape (dotted lines) from center and make a white or yellow paper buckle.

Name _____

1 – red
2 – yellow
3 – blue
4 – green
5 – orange

6 – purple
7 – brown
8 – light brown
9 – light blue

Color the corn kernels red, yellow, blue, and purple.

97

December Contents

Sunday	Monday	Tuesday	Wednesday	Thursday	Friday	Saturday

December Birthdays

5	Martin Van Buren	8th president; first president to be born a citizen of the United States
6	Ira Gershwin	American lyricist
	Joyce Kilmer	poet; "Trees"
10	Melvil Dewey	librarian; invented decimal cataloging system
	Emily Dickinson	great 19th century poet, American
16	Ludwig van Beethoven	great orchestral composer; German
	Margaret Mead	American anthropologist, author, speaker
24	Kit Carson	American frontiersman, trail guide
25	Clara Barton	founder of the American Red Cross
	Sir Isaac Newton	English mathematician and scientist
26	Mao Tse-tung	founded the People's Republic of China in 1949
27	Louis Pasteur	French chemist-bacteriologist; milk pasteurization; developed anthrax vaccine and first vaccine for rabies
	Radio City Music Hall	1932; world's largest indoor theatre
28	Woodrow Wilson	28th president
29	Andrew Johnson	17th president
30	Rudyard Kipling	English poet, novelist; *The Jungle Book*

Alexander and the Bill of Rights

Now Alexander, listen to me,
I'm going to talk about history.

Amendments were added to our constitution,
Fifteen years after the revolution.

The first ten of these are special indeed,
They protect the rights U.S. citizens need.

This first bill of Rights still helps you and me,
To live happily in the land of the free.

Now, no more rhymes until we are done,
For I want you to learn about each one!

(So turn the page and you will hear,
about these rights we hold so dear.)

1. Freedom of religion, speech, the press, and the right to peaceably assemble (demonstrate).

2. Citizens have the right to keep and bear arms.

3. The government cannot use your house for soldiers to live there.

4. There must be a very good reason (and a warrant) to search your house, yourself or your possessions.

TSD 2365-8 *The Elementary Calendar*

5 You do not have to "tell" about something criminal you may have done.

6 You have the right to a lawyer to help you, a jury, and a "speedy and public" trial.

I. M. A. LAWYER

7 You have the right to a trial by jury.

8 Bail and fines may not be too high; punishment may not be "cruel or unusual."

TSD 2365-8 *The Elementary Calendar*

9 You have other rights besides those in the Constitution.

10 Each state and the people have powers, too (unless the Constitution states otherwise).

And there they are; the rules—all ten,
That have kept us safe again and again.

Remember your rights, Alexander, my dear.
They make it safe for us to live here.

TSD 2365-8 *The Elementary Calendar*

Name _____

Holiday Food Pyramid

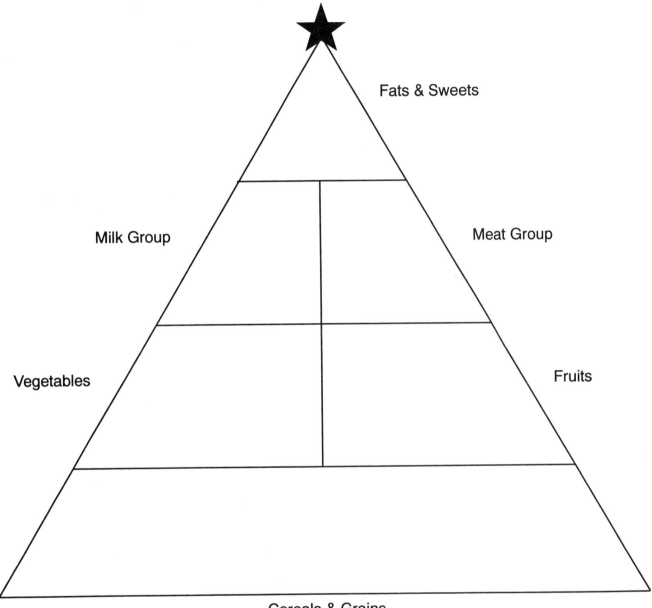

The Food Pyramid looks a little like a Christmas tree!
Write the names of these holiday foods in the correct spaces on the tree.

rice   ham
peas   cheese
fruit cup   stuffing
turkey   milk
bread   cranberries
carrots   crackers
potatoes   ice cream

TSD 2365-8 *The Elementary Calendar*

Holiday Foods

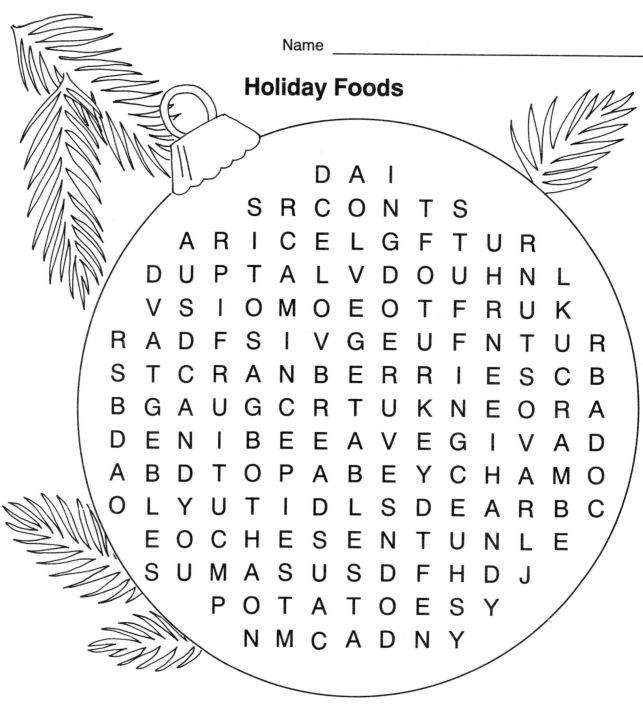

```
        D A I
      S R C O N T S
    A R I C E L G F T U R
  D U P T A L V D O U H N L
  V S I O M O E O T F R U K
R A D F S I V G E U F N T U R
S T C R A N B E R R I E S C B
B G A U G C R T U K N E O R A
D E N I B E E A V E G I V A D
A B D T O P A B E Y C H A M O
O L Y U T I D L S D E A R B C
  E O C H E S E N T U N L E
  S U M A S U S D F H D J
    P O T A T O E S Y
      N M C A D N Y
```

Fill in the correct word, then find it in the puzzle. (Hint: Use the puzzle for spelling help.)

1. A favorite holiday bird: _____

2. These can be baked, mashed, or sweet: _____

3. Round and red, string them or make them into sauce: _____

Find these other holiday favorites in the puzzle.

STUFFING	MINCE PIE	NUTS
CANDY	FRUIT	RICE
VEGETABLES	BREADS	HAM

Merry Christmas From . . .

France	Joyeux Noël
Italy	Buone Feste Natalizie
Spain	Feliz Navidad
Holland	Vrolyk Kerstfeest
Ireland	Nodlaig Mhaith Chugnat
Denmark	Glaedelig Jul
Norway	God Jul
Poland	Boze Narodzenie
Germany	Froehliche Weihnachten
Puerto Rico	Felices Pascuas
Japan	Meri Kurisumasu
China	Kung Hsi Hsin Nien

The Christmas Story

Long, long ago a young woman named Mary lived in Nazareth. One day an angel appeared to tell Mary that she had been chosen to be the mother of Jesus, the Son of God. The man Mary was going to marry, a carpenter named Joseph, was to be Jesus' father on earth.

When it was almost time for the baby to be born, Mary and Joseph set out for Bethlehem. The emperor of Rome had ordered that every man must return to the place of his birth to pay a tax. Joseph had been born in Bethlehem.

Mary rode on Joseph's sturdy little donkey, but when they reached Bethlehem she was very tired. She knew the baby would be born soon and she asked Joseph to find a place for them to stay for the birth. However, so many people had come to Bethlehem to pay the emperor's tax, that all the inns were filled and there was not one room for Mary and Joseph.

At last a little girl told them they might be able to stay in the stable of her parents' inn. The stable was clean, warm, and dry. Mary and Joseph were glad to rest after their long journey. Soon the baby was born and Mary remembered to call him Jesus as the angel had instructed her. She wrapped the baby warmly and laid him in a manger filled with clean, soft hay.

That night, an angel appeared to shepherds guarding their sheep in the fields near Bethlehem. The angel told the shepherds the good news of Jesus' birth and put a bright star in the sky to lead them to the stable. They followed the star as it moved toward the city, and when they found Jesus in the stable, the shepherds knelt to thank God for sending his Son to save the world.

Three kings from the East also saw the star and followed it to Bethlehem, bringing gifts for the Holy One. One king brought gold; one brought frankincense; and the third brought myrrh. They told Mary that Jesus, too, would be a king. He would be the King of Heaven.

Today people in many parts of the world celebrate the birth of Jesus. They call it Christmas and try to make it a happy time of peace on earth and good will toward one another.

manger: a box to hold feed for cattle
frankincense: incense
myrrh: sap from the myrrha plant used
    to make perfume or incense

Christmas Customs

The Tree

Long, long ago the Egyptians and Romans brought trees indoors and decorated them. They were a symbol of new life in the world after the long, dark winter. When Christianity began to spread, the custom of the tree was kept. Later, Martin Luther decorated a tree with candles for his children, and the custom soon spread to other countries.

Two German folk tales explain how the tree came to be decorated. In the first, a woodsman and his family take in a little boy from the cold winter night and give him food and a place to sleep. The next morning the singing of angels awakens the family and they realize that the little boy is the Christ child. To repay them for their kindness, the child touches a little fir tree in their yard and says, "May this tree glow to warm your hearts and carry presents for you."

In the second story, a widow decorates a tree for her children. During the night spiders spin webs all over it. The Christ child turns the webs to silver, and that is why we use tinsel on our trees today.

Candles and Lights

Christmas candles and lights are a combination of Roman and Hebrew customs. For the Romans, lights symbolized the return of the sun to the world after the winter. The Jewish "Feast of Lights" (Hanukkah) celebrates religious freedom. Christians believe that Christ is the "Light of the World." In many countries candles are placed in the windows at Christmas to help the Christ child find his way. Outdoor lights and tree lights brighten the Christmas holiday.

Stars

The stars we see at Christmas symbolize the star in the East that Christians believe led the shepherds and wise men to Bethlehem long ago.

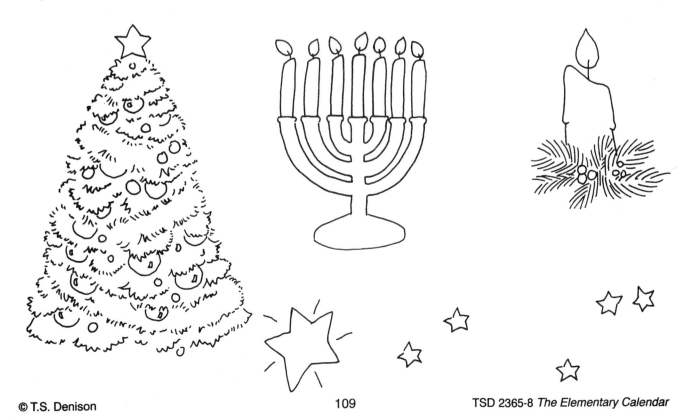

Poinsettias

Long ago in Mexico, there was a poor girl who had no gift to take to the church at Christmastime. An angel carved from stone came to life and told the girl to gather some of the weeds that grew at the base of the statue and take them as her gift. As the little girl walked down the aisle of the church, the top leaves of the plants turned a beautiful red.

The beautiful red and green plant that has become our Christmas flower is called the "fire flower" in Mexico. It was brought to this country by a United States official named Poinsett, which is how it got its name here.

Stockings

Long ago in Holland, Saint Nicholas threw purses of gold down the chimney of a poor man's house so that the man's daughters could marry. The purses fell into stockings that were hung by the fire to dry.

Santa Claus

In the Netherlands, Saint Nicholas, the patron saint of children, is called Sinterklaas. We pronounce it Santa Claus. Many countries have a kind old man who comes to visit good children at Christmastime. In Germany he is Kris Kringle and in France, Père Noël. In other lands he is Father Christmas.

Holly, Mistletoe, and Greens

There is a story that a tiny lamb scratched himself on holly branches as he made his way to the stable in Bethlehem. His young shepherd picked him up to comfort him. Mary saw this and told the shepherd that her son, too, would be kind to animals.

In England, mistletoe has always been a symbol of friendship. Enemies who meet under it stop fighting; good friends renew their friendship; and today, a person standing under the mistletoe can expect a kiss!

Bringing pine and fir branches into the house is an old custom. They bring new life and a pleasant smell to a closed, winter house.

Animals

The animals in the stable gave gifts to the Holy Child, too. The sheep gave wool; the cow gave up her hay and breathed on the baby to keep Him warm; the dove sang a lullaby. Some people believe that on Christmas Eve the animals can talk, but since it is bad luck to disturb them on this special night, no one has ever heard them.

Nativity Scene

A Nativity scene is an arrangement of figures to show the stable and manger where Christ was born. It can be very simple or very elaborate. In Italy the scene is called the presepio; in Spain it is the pesebre and in France it is called a crèche. Saint Francis of Assisi brought back the idea from a visit to Bethlehem in 1224 and set up a manger scene in the town of Greccio in Italy. Soon the nativity was popular all over Europe.

Bells

Bells announce the beginning of the Christmas celebration on Christmas Eve. In the Netherlands, Saint Nicholas carries a hand bell on his visits. Today they have become part of our decorations as well as part of our religious services.

The Yule Log

A fire in the hearth is a symbol of home and safety because it gives warmth and light. The yule log is a Scandinavian tradition that has become popular in England. In some places the Christmas celebration lasts as long as the log will glow and that is why the yule log is so enormous.

Advent Calendars, Candles, and Wreaths

Everyone likes to count the days until Christmas. The period of the twenty-four days before Christmas is called Advent. The four Sundays before Christmas are called Advent Sundays. An Advent calendar is often a cardboard house with twenty-four windows that open; one for each day before Christmas. In the window is a Christmas verse or a small gift. Advent candles are set on a narrow board that is raised at one end. One candle is lighted on the first Advent Sunday, two on the second, and so on. There is a larger candle at the end for Christmas Day. Advent wreaths also hold gifts or candles.

Carols

Carols began as songs to celebrate the birth of the Christ child and to carry the message of the Christmas season. They are sung for the same reasons today.

Gifts

The gifts that are exchanged today symbolize the gifts that were offered to the Christ child long ago in Bethlehem.

Christmas in . . .

Great Britain

Christmas is celebrated in Great Britain very much as it is in the United States, with many customs borrowed from other countries around the world. Before Christmas, British children enjoy caroling and decorating the house with holly and mistletoe. In England, mistletoe has been a symbol of friendship for many years.

On Christmas Eve children hang stockings over the fireplace or at the ends of their beds, so when Santa Claus arrives driving his sleigh and wearing a long red robe, he can fill the stockings with small presents. A handsome yule log is lighted in the fireplace.

On Christmas Day gifts are exchanged with relatives and friends and the family gathers for a wonderful feast of roast ham, puddings, and mincemeat pies. If a plum pudding is served, it is coated with brandy and lighted so that it comes to the table flaming.

In Ireland, candles are placed in the windows to welcome wanderers and to welcome the Holy family if they should pass. In Wales, caroling is an important part of the Christmas season. In Scotland, the main family celebration is held on New Year's Eve which is called Hogmanay.

United States

People from many countries around the world have come to live in the United States and they have brought their Christmas customs with them. Americans enjoy the yule log from Scandanavia and Great Britain; poinsettias from Mexico; the decorated tree from Germany, and nativity scenes from Italy and France. Santa Claus must have stopped in Denmark to pick up a few *nissen* on his way to America because now the busy little elves work for him.

Christmas in . . .

Norway – Sweden – Finland – Denmark

In Scandinavian countries Christmas preparations begin early. The streets are decorated with greenery and lights. Gifts in shopwindows are decorated with fir sprigs, hearts, or stars. Homes and barns are cleaned from top to bottom and families bake for the coming holiday.

Christmas elves begin to appear in newspapers, magazines, cards, ornaments, and toys. In Denmark, the elves are called *nissen*. They live in country barns and come out to help ring the bells on Christmas Eve. They are very kind if you treat them well, but if you make them angry they cause a lot of trouble—upsetting, spilling, and hiding things. A favorite decoration in Denmark is a white village church set in a glittering snow scene with tiny *nissen* sledding around it.

Straw, to remind people of the manger in Bethlehem, is an important part of Scandinavian celebrations. It is spread on the floor in some places and it is used to make ornaments in many shapes.

On Christmas Eve the tree is lighted after dinner. It is decorated with the straw ornaments, paper heart baskets filled with candy, small flags, bells, fruit, candy, and tinsel. Santa and his elves (the helpful *nissen*) may deliver gifts in person. In Denmark Santa looks a lot like Dad.

On Scandinavian farms it is also important to share the Christmas festivities with the animals. Corn, nuts, suet, and grain are put out for the birds. The farm animals are given extra feed, and of course, the tiny barn elf is given a treat, too.

In Sweden, December 13 is Saint Lucia's Day. A daughter of the house plays the part of Saint Lucia. She delivers coffee and buns to the rest of the family for breakfast. This represents Saint Lucia who delivered food to the early Christians. The girl wears a white dress with a red sash and a crown of pine boughs and seven lit candles.

Christmas Day is a time for church services and quiet family activities. On December 26, friends and neighbors visit each other for parties and good food.

Paper Heart Baskets

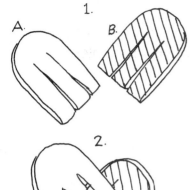

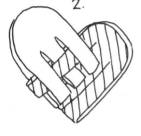

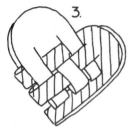

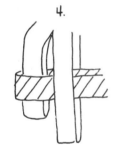

Materials: 9" x 12" (229 x 305 mm) red and white paper, scissors, glue

Cut paper in half lengthwise. Use different colors—red and white are traditional. Make sure each child has two strips in two *different* colors.

Fold each strip in half. Round off the open corners and make two long, evenly-spaced slits from the folded edge (figure 1).

Leaving the paper folded, begin weaving the "legs" through and into one another: A through B, B through A, and A through B again. When the first two legs have been woven through, push them up and weave the last one through the bottom (figures 2 and 3).

The weaving is difficult the first time and requires some bending, folding, and fiddling with the paper loops or legs. Try it yourself first before doing it with the children (figure 4).

When the basket is finished, add a paper handle for hanging, and fill the basket with small candies.

Done in red and white, this makes a great Valentine's Day project.

Straw Ornaments

This project imitates the straw ornaments popular in Scandanavia.

Materials: paper craft straws, string, glue

Tie paper craft straws or drinking straws (6" or 152 mm is a good length) into bundles. Spread the ends and fasten the bundles together to make the shapes below, or invent a design of your own. Try different straw lengths.

Cut the gathered straws into shapes (center figure) *after* they have been tied. (A little glue is helpful.) Cut the ends into points if desired.

Christmas in . . .

Spain

In Spain the *pesebre* (nativity scene) is decorated with candles and filled with familiar figures; women washing clothes in a stream, a Spanish bull, and even *toreadors* (bullfighters).

After midnight mass on Christmas Eve, families gather for the *cena de Nochebuena*, the dinner of the Good Day. After dinner everyone sings hymns and carols around the tree.

On the night of January 5, children fill their shoes with hay to feed the camels of the three wise men. When the children wake up in the morning, their shoes are filled with gifts.

Mexico

Mexican homes are decorated with Spanish moss, greenery, and paper lanterns to prepare for the *posadas* which begin on December 16 and continue for nine days. For each *posada*, children candles and a board with clay nativity figures from house to house, singing as they look for a resting place, or *posada*, just as Mary and Joseph did so long ago. They are told there is no room again and again until one house welcomes them into the living room. There, everyone says prayers of thanks and celebrates with food and fireworks.

At the party, there are *piñatas* for the children. A clay jar in the shape of a bull, bird, or doll is filled with candy and sealed with paper at the bottom. It is decorated with fancy tissue frills and streamers, then hung where it can swing freely. Blindfolded children try to break the *piñata* with a stick so that the candy falls out. All the children scramble to collect it.

The last *posada* is on Christmas Eve. After prayers, the baby Jesus is placed in the manger of the nativity scene. Midnight mass is followed by church bells ringing in the happy time and by more fireworks.

On January 5, Mexican children follow the Spanish custom of putting out their shoes for the three wise men to fill during the night.

Puerto Rico

Today many Puerto Rican homes have Christmas trees and visits from Santa Claus, but children still fill boxes with river grasses and put them out on January 5, for the three kings to fill with gifts. On January 6, the kings, in fancy costumes, visit houses to deliver gifts of fruit and candy. On January 6, 7, and 8, neighbors and friends visit each others' homes to share the holiday spirit.

January 12 is Bethlehem day. Three children dressed as the wise men ride ponies and lead a procession of angels and shepherds playing flutes and carrying gifts for the infant Jesus. It is an honor for children to take part in the Bethlehem Day procession.

Christmas in . . .

France

Children in France look forward to December 6, Saint Nicholas Day, when they receive candy and gifts. Saint Nicholas Day marks the beginning of the Christmas season. At home they help to place the figures in the *crèche* (nativity scene) and decorate the tree with candles, tinsel, and many colored stars. They admire the big cherry yule log that burns in the fireplace. It is a custom in France to leave the fire and the candles burning to welcome Mary and Jesus in case they should visit.

On Christmas Eve everyone goes to midnight mass and afterward the family has a late supper called the réveillon. The children set out their shoes on the hearth to wait for Père Noël. During the night Père Noël fills the shoes with presents and hangs candy, fruit, and toys on the tree.

On Christmas Day there are more religious services and afterward, huge family feasts for everyone to enjoy.

Italy

In Italy the celebration of Christmas begins on December 16 and lasts until January 6 (Epiphany or Three Kings Day). The *presepio*, or manger scene, is the center of the celebration in every town and every home. There are live performances of the Christmas story and each town tries to make its *presepio* display bigger and more beautiful than that of the next town. The custom of the *presepio* was brought to Italy by Saint Francis of Assisi many years ago.

It is an old Italian custom for children, dressed as shepherds, to go from house to house playing pipes and reciting. They collect money to spend for Christmas.

For twenty-four hours before Christmas, no one eats. Then, after midnight mass on Christmas Eve, there is an enormous feast with *panetone*, a Christmas cake.

Presents do not arrive until Three Kings Day (January 6) when the good witch, Befana, comes down the chimney to leave gifts in good children's shoes, but charcoal for bad children.

Christmas in . . .

Germany
Germany is the land of Christmas trees and beautiful hand-made toys. Martin Luther introduced the fir tree decorated with candles many years ago and its popularity spread throughout Europe.

In Germany, the mother is in charge of decorating the tree with tinsel, glass balls, and cookies shaped like hearts, animals, and stars. The family is not allowed to see the tree until six o'clock on Christmas Eve when everyone rushes into the living room to admire it.

Advent wreaths are popular in Germany. The wreath may be hung with twenty-four tiny gifts, one to open every day during the twenty-four days of Advent, or it may lie flat and hold four candles. One candle is lighted on the first Advent Sunday, two on the second, and so on until Christmas Day.

German children receive their gifts from the *Christkind* or Christ child. He wears a white robe and has gold wings and a gold crown. Santa visits, too, but he is in charge of reporting the children's behavior to see whether they should receive gifts or birch rods.

The Netherlands
The Netherlands has given us Santa Claus. He is Saint Nicholas, patron saint of children, and *Sinterklass* in Dutch. He and his servant, Black Peter, come to Amsterdam on a boat from Spain, on December 6. He wears red robes and rides a white horse to lead a parade into the city. Black Peter carries a book with the names of good and bad children listed in it for Saint Nicholas to see.

Sometimes Sinterklass flies over the rooftops to give out presents. Shoes filled with hay for his horse are left by the fire to be stuffed with candy during the night. Gifts are also left on a table and on the hearth.

On Christmas Day, families gather for church services and feasts with special foods.

Christmas in . . .

Poland

On Christmas Eve in Poland, children watch very carefully for the first star to appear in the night sky so that the Christmas feast may begin. Before they eat, the family passes an *oplatek* around the table so everyone may have a piece. An *oplatek* is a thin bread wafer with a picture of Mary, Joseph, and Jesus stamped on it. Pets are given a small piece, too.

Hay is spread on the floor and even under the tablecloth so that people may remember that Jesus was born in a manger. Two places are left at the table, one for Mary and one for Jesus. At this Christmas Eve feast, there must always be an even number of places at the table and an odd number of foods— fish, poppy seed noodles, sauerkraut dumplings, cookies, fruit, nuts, and cakes.

After dinner the family lights the tree, gifts are exchanged and carols sung. Then the family attends a midnight church service.

Russia

Religious holidays were forbidden after the Russian Revolution, however, many customs remain.

The tree is called a New Year's tree and Santa Claus is Grandfather Frost. *Kolyada* (Father Christmas) may also visit.

There is a fast before Christmas Eve services, no one eats for many hours before going to church. The local priest comes to bless the house with holy water.

In December of 1991, Russia's communist government fell and a democratic government came into power. Now that Russia is no longer a communist country perhaps more traditional Christmas celebrations will occur.

Christmas in . . .

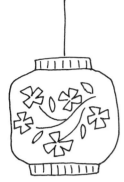

China
Although most people in China are not Christians and do not celebrate Christmas, many have adopted the bright decorations of the holiday and added pretty lanterns. Gifts may be exchanged on Christmas Day, with expensive gifts for the family, and food or flowers for other relatives and friends.

Chinese Christians celebrate Christmas western style. *Lan Khoong* (Nice Old Father) or *Dun Che Lao Ren* (Christmas Old Man) fills stockings and brings gifts.

A more important holiday is the Chinese New Year (in January or February by the western calendar). That is when children receive new clothes and toys, and enjoy feasts of special foods and fireworks displays.

Japan
In Japan many western customs are celebrated at Christmas even though most people are not Christians. There are Christmas trees and decorations of paper holly and bells and the stores hold Christmas sales. Christmas cards are exchanged and there are children's parties with presents, games, and Christmas cake.

India
In India most people are Hindu or Moslem. There are a few Christians there who decorate banana or mango trees since there are no fir trees. They decorate their homes with mango leaves. Small clay oil lamps burn on flat roof edges, and churches are decorated with candles and poinsettias.

Iran
Iran used to be called Persia. It is the home of the Magi (three kings) who followed the bright star to the stable in Bethlehem. Most people in Iran are Moslems, not Christians. For the few Christians, Christmas is the "Little Feast" and Easter is "The Greatest Feast." Children may receive new clothes, but there is no Santa Claus and no gifts are exchanged.

Iraq
On Christmas Eve Iraqi Christians light a bonfire of dried thorns. If all the thorns burn to ash it means good fortune for the coming year. Each person in the family jumps over the ashes three times and makes a wish. On Christmas day a fire is lit in the church and the bishop carries an image of Jesus on a red velvet cushion. He touches one member of the congregation who touches another and so on to spread "The touch of peace."

December Dates

3 ***Maulid al Nabi***—birthday of the prophet, Muhammad; first day of Rabi I on the Islamic Calendar. People wear new clothes and gather with family and friends to exchange gifts.

6 ***Saint Nicholas Day*** in France, Germany, Switzerland, and the Netherlands.

11 ***Birthday of UNICEF***—United Nations International Children's Emergency Fund which helps children in developing nations.

12 ***La Virgen de Guadalupe***—thousands of Mexicans come to honor the Virgin of Guadalupe in a church built on the spot where they believe Mary appeared to an Indian woodcutter and caused roses to grow out of season.

12 Thirteen mischievous Christmas Men of Iceland begin visiting homes, one a day, until Christmas. They are never seen, but each one leaves a gift and a sign of his arrival. Candle Beggar may take a few candles and Meat Hooker (by dangling a hood down the chimney) may steal the Christmas roast. Guess what trick Door Slammer plays!

13 ***Saint Lucia's Day*** in Sweden

16 ***Posadas*** begins in Mexico

17 ***Klöpfelnächte***—"knocking nights," the three Thursdays before Christmas. Children wear masks and go from house to house chanting rhymes which begin with "knock" and cracking whips, ringing cow bells, and clattering pots to drive away evil spirits. They are given fruit, candy, or coins.

18 ***Misa de Aquinaldo***—In Caracas, Venezuela, people rollerskate to this Christmas carol mass!

21 ***Mayan Pole Dance***—Mayan Indians in Mexico honor the Sun God with the dangerous pole dance. Two men climb to a fifty-foot high platform and wind a rope tightly to one foot. They jump from the platform. If they land on their feet, the Sun God will shine a little longer each day.

22 ***Incwala Kingship Ceremony***—in Swaziland, Africa, warriors dance around their King (who has been hiding himself), begging him to come back to his people. Finally, the king agrees. He dances the king's dance and eats part of a pumpkin to show that everyone may join him in the harvest feast.

23 ***Night of the Radishes***—In Oaxaca, Mexico, radishes can grow as long as a child's arm. People carve them into sculptures and the best one wins a prize.

24 ***Christmas Eve***—the day before Jesus' birth

25 ***Christmas Day***—Christians throughout the world celebrate the birth of Jesus

26 ***Saint Stephen's Day***—to honor the first Christian martyr. Boxing Day in England when servants and tradesmen are given "boxes" containing a gift or money.

27 ***Ta Chiu***—festival of peace and renewal in Hong Kong. All gods and ghosts are gathered in one place and honored. A list of the names of everyone in the area is attached to a paper horse and burned so it will rise to heaven.

29 ***Kulig***—a winter sleigh party in Poland. Firecrackers are thrown and children tumble in the snow. A hearty supper is cooked over a fire in the woods.

31 ***New Year's Eve***

Hanukkah

The story of Hanukkah is more than 2000 years old. At that time a wicked king ruled the Jewish Holy Land. He ordered the people to worship the idols he placed in their temple instead of their own God. The Jewish people rebelled and, led by the heroic Maccabees, they fought a long and terrible war against the king's army.

After many years of fighting, the Jewish people drove out the enemy. They threw the idols out of their temple and cleaned and repaired it. Then they started to light the lamp that burns all day and all night in every temple. They were horrified to find that there was only enough oil to keep the lamp burning for one day. They knew that it would take eight days to make more oil. Sadly, they lighted the little lamp. An amazing thing happened! The little bit of oil kept the lamp burning for eight days—until the new oil was ready.

Today Hanukkah is a joyous "Feast of Lights" to celebrate the miracle of the long-ago lamp. It is celebrated on the twenty-fifth day of the Jewish month of *Kislev*, usually in December. A candle holder called a menorah holds nine candles. Each day for eight days the center candle is used to light one more candle until all eight are burning.

Hanukkah is a time for family gatherings, feasting, games, and giving gifts. Frying foods in oil is a reminder of the Hanukkah miracle and everyone enjoys potato *latkes* (pancakes) served with sour cream and apple sauce; *kreplach*, a dumpling filled with meat or cheese; a fried pastry called *strudel*; and doughnuts, which are popular in Israel today. There are also cookies baked in popular shapes.

While the adults play chess and cards, or enjoy riddles, word games, and number games, children play with the *dreidel*. The *dreidel* is a four-sided top with a Hebrew letter on each side. Tokens of candy, nuts, chips, or some other small item are put into a center kitty and children take turns spinning the *dreidel*. When the *dreidel* stops and falls, they must follow the direction given by the letter on the top side. If it is *nun*, they must do nothing or pass; if it is *gimel*, they take all of the kitty and a new one must be put in; if it is *he,* they may take half the kity; and if it is *shin*, they must pay the kitty an amount decided upon before the game began. The game ends when someone has won all the tokens or by the child who has the most tokens when everyone tires of the game.

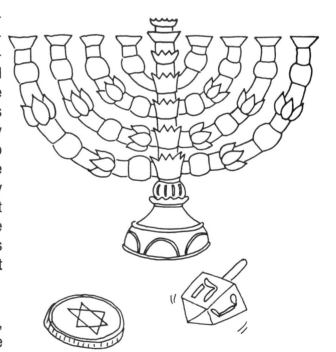

Hanukkah *gelt* is a traditional gift. Money or coins, the *gelt* is a symbol of the first coins made by the long ago Jews when they won their freedom. Often children are given a small gift on each night of the holiday as the candle is lighted in the menorah.

Kwanzaa

Kwanzaa is an African-American holiday begun in 1966 by a college professor and black activist named Maulana Karenga to celebrate African heritage and culture. Although Kwanzaa begins on December 26 and lasts through New Year's Day, it has nothing to do with Christmas. The ideas for Kwanzaa came from African farming festivals which celebrate the first harvest of the season. In Swahili, *Matunda ya Kwanzaa* means "first fruits of the season."

On each day of the seven days of Kwanzaa, a candle is lighted in a holder called a *kinara*. There are three red candles, three green ones and one black one. These are the colors for all Kwanzaa decorations; they symbolize black unity and pride. The candles also stand for the seven principles of Kwanzaa. Each day, young people are asked *"Habari gani?"* They answer with the principle of that day.

Each principle comes from an African saying:

1. *Umoja* (Unity) "When spider webs join they can tie up a lion."
   Unity of the family, the community, the nation, and the race
2. *Kujichagulia* (Self-determination) "No matter how full the river, it still wants to grow."
   Personal growth, learning and values
3. *Ujima* (Collective work and responsibility) "When two elephants fight, only the grass will suffer."
   Working together with each person doing her/his job
4. *Ujamaa* (Cooperative economics) "A brother is like one's shoulder."
   Making and spending money, working together for mutual benefit
5. *Nia* (Purpose) "He who learns teaches."
   Developing and sharing skills and abilities
6. *Kuumba* (Creativity) "A tall tree is the pride of the forest."
   Developing creative talents
7. *Imani* (Faith) "He who cannot dance says the drum is all bad."
   Understanding and passing along African heritage

Things for the Kwanzaa celebration are placed on a *mkeka* (straw mat): corn, gifts, and a unity cup. The family drinks from the cup, gives thanks, and exchanges gifts. On the sixth night (New Year's Eve) there is a Kwanzaa *karamu* (feast) with special foods, songs, dances, and stories about African culture and heritage.

Kwanzaa gifts are often educational (books), handmade, or inexpensive. They usually have something to do with one of the seven principles.

BE A DEAR AND...

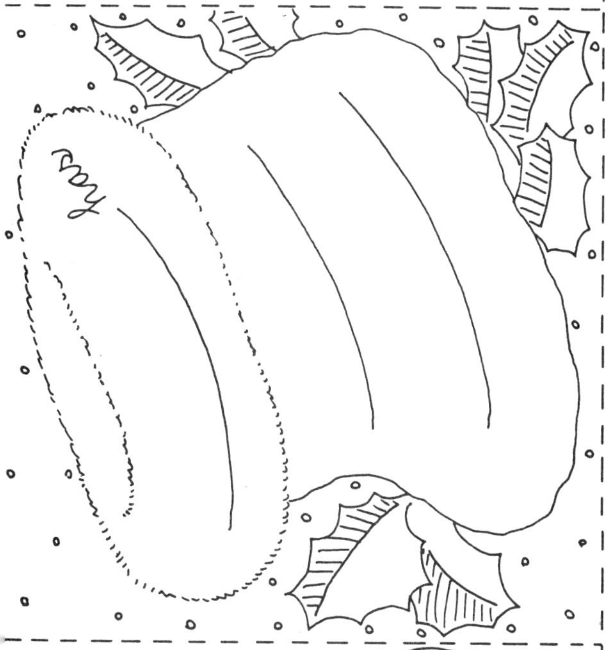

Sweet Kid Award

for

Good Work December

Star of the Day

Holiday Word Search

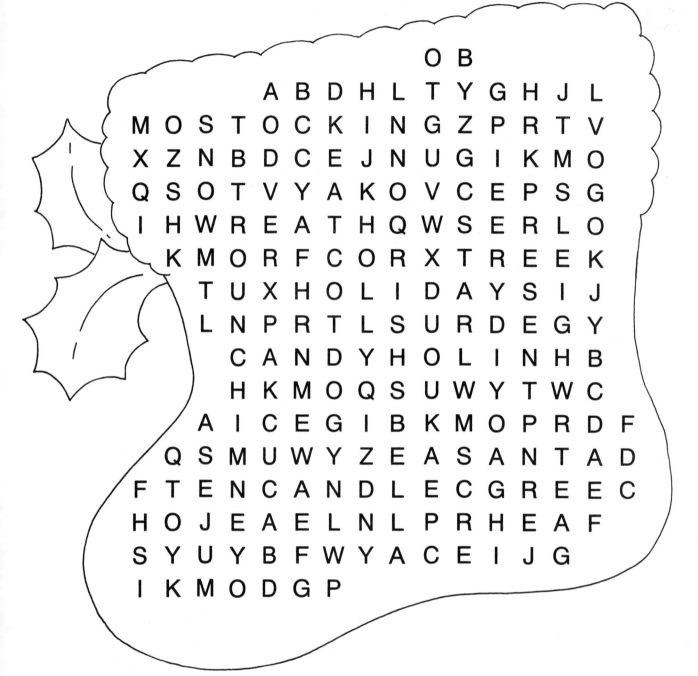

Circle the words hidden in the Christmas stocking.

HOLIDAY	WREATH	STAR
CANDLE	SANTA	STOCKING
BELL	PRESENT	CHIMNEY
HOLLY	TOY	CANDY
TREE	SLEIGH	SNOW

1. Write a math problem in each present. Write the corresponding answer in a tag.
2. Mask these directions and print your own before copying.

Name _____

Present Pyramid

Visions of Sugarplums . . .

Fill the space above with words or pictures to show what the little boy is dreaming. Color the page.

Stained Glass

Materials: colored cellophane, aluminum foil

Draw frame on 12" x 15" (305 x 390 mm) black construction paper. (The width of a ruler works easily.)

Draw a large, simple design inside the frame. Make sure the design is attached to the frame at some points on all four sides.

Double all lines to form bands as shown.

Cut away the background, carefully inserting scissors to avoid cutting the frame.

Back with a suitable color of cellophane. Lightly crumple aluminum foil, flatten, and place behind cellophane.

Staple frame, cellophane, and foil together. *(White glue does not work well since both cellophane and foil resist it.)*

Trim away cellophane and foil around edges of frame.

Fireplace

Materials: red and white construction paper, aluminum foil or glitter

Cut fireplace opening from front. (Make sure only front of card is cut.)

Cut and glue a white strip for the mantel. Draw bricks with marker or crayon.

Let students decorate fireplace as they wish, adding stockings, greenery, and decorations cut from scraps of construction paper.

Cut out and glue "fire" to inside back of card; use foil or glitter. Add touches of "fire" on the front if desired. Write a message inside.

Santa Card Holder

Materials: 12" x 18" (305 x 457 mm) and 9" x 12" (229 x 305 mm) red construction paper, 6" (152 mm) square pink construction paper, 1½" x 12" (39 x 305 mm) black construction paper, pieces of cotton, 9"(229 mm) or 12" (305 mm) paper plates, scissors, glue, glitter

Trace the paper plate on the 12" x 18" (305 x 457 mm) red construction paper.

Draw a long triangle for the hat on the remaining red paper. Cut out and save all scraps.

Use plate again to trace a half circle on long edge of 9" x 12" (229 x 305 mm) red paper. Cut out.

Glue black strip to straight edge of half circle. Trim excess from the back and save.

Dot glue on curved edge of half circle only and glue to circle, forming pocket.

Cut corners from 6" (152 mm) square pink paper for face (it does not have to be round) and glue to edge of circle above pocket, making sure that Santa is right side up!

Glue the long triangular hat made earlier to the top of head. Bring down point and fasten with small piece of cotton as shown.

Pull and stretch remaining cotton very thin and glue around face and bottom of hat.

From red scraps make circles for nose and cheeks. From black scraps cut off two corners for eyes.

Draw buckle or child's name with glue on belt. Sprinkle with glitter.

Pop-Up

Materials: 6" x 9" (152 x 229 mm) or 9" x 12" (229 x 305 mm) white construction paper or tagboard, markers or crayons, scissors

Fold paper or tagboard in half lightly. Open.

Design Christmas card on lower half of paper. Allow some objects to cross above center fold line. Keep these objects ½"(13 mm) from side of card. Color card with markers or crayons.

Insert scissors carefully to cut around objects above fold. Stand card as shown.

Unless paper is very stiff, keep pop-ups low or fold paper the long way.

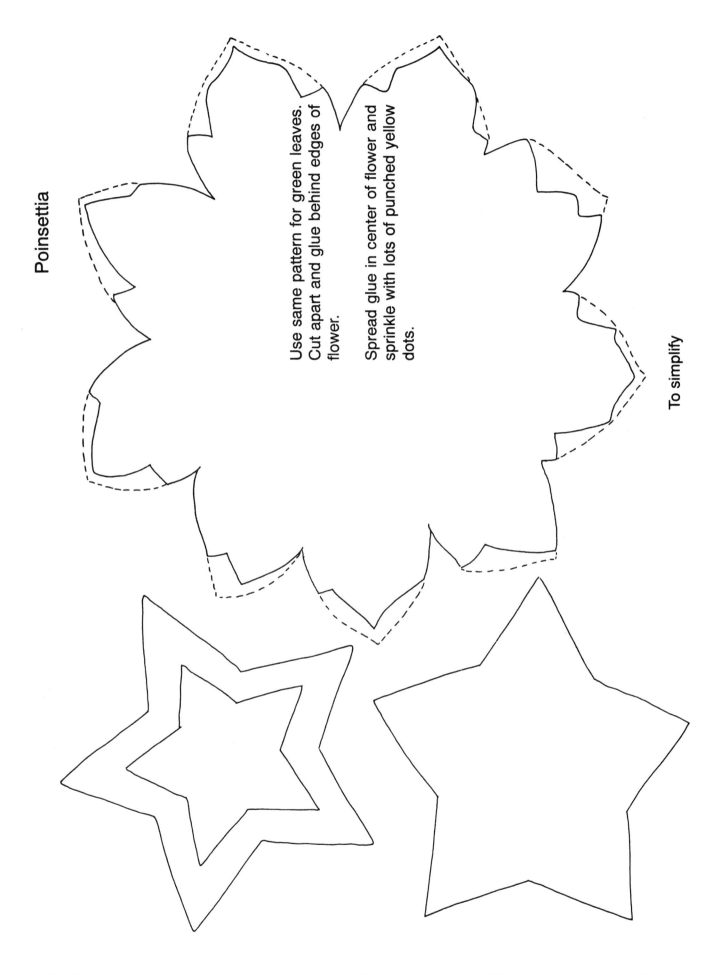

Poinsettia

Use same pattern for green leaves. Cut apart and glue behind edges of flower.

Spread glue in center of flower and sprinkle with lots of punched yellow dots.

To simplify

TSD 2365-8 *The Elementary Calendar*

Have children decorate tree with small stickers (stars, dots, crescents, etc.) or paper punch dots.

Fold a 2" x 18" (52 x 457 mm) strip of colored paper without creasing it. Staple together along with the top bell (as shown). Staple or glue more bells and holly.

Speedy Bows

1) Fold two long rectangles (twice the width of the bow) together.
2) Cut as shown.
3) Clip triangle from open ends of one folded rectangle. Open pieces and arrange bow as shown. Use scraps for center.

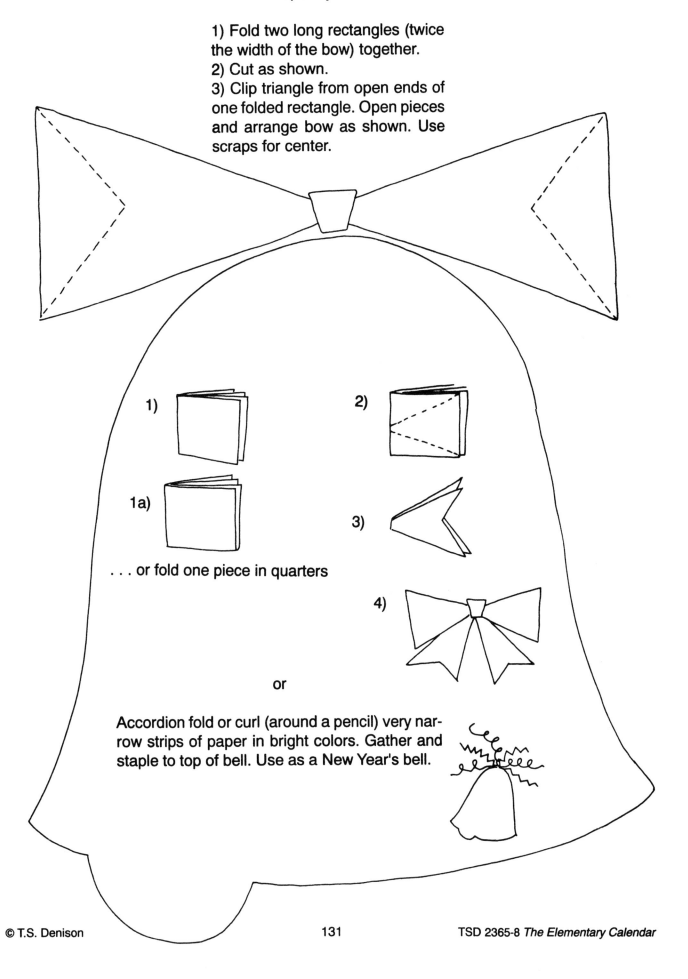

1)

2)

1a)

3)

. . . or fold one piece in quarters

4)

or

Accordion fold or curl (around a pencil) very narrow strips of paper in bright colors. Gather and staple to top of bell. Use as a New Year's bell.

                                       TSD 2365-8 *The Elementary Calendar*

Name _____

0 – white
1 – red
2 – yellow
3 – blue
4 – green
5 – orange

6 – purple
7 – brown
8 – black
9 – pink
10 – light blue

Color any remaining spaces however you like.

TSD 2365-8 *The Elementary Calendar*

January Contents

Sunday	Monday	Tuesday	Wednesday	Thursday	Friday	Saturday

TSD 2365-8 *The Elementary Calendar*

JANUARY BIRTHDAYS

1 Paul Revere — patriot; silversmith; famous for "Midnight Ride"
    Betsy Ross — first stars and stripes flag, 1775

4 Louis Braille — invented Braille system of reading and writing

6 Carl Sandburg — American poet; biographer; historian; folklorist

7 Millard Fillmore — 13th president

9 Richard M. Nixon — 37th president; resigned August 9, 1974

11 Alexander Hamilton — American statesman (exact birth date unknown)

14 Albert Schweitzer — philosopher; musician; physician; scientist

15 Martin Luther King, Jr. — minister; civil rights leader, assassinated April 4, 1968

18 Daniel Webster — American statesman; orator; lawyer
    Pooh Day — birthday of children's author A.A. Milne

19 Robert E. Lee — general in chief of all Confederate armies
    Edgar Allan Poe — American poet and storywriter; *The Raven*

21 Stonewall Jackson — Jonathan "Stonewall" Jackson, famous Confederate general

23 John Hancock — first of the Declaration of Independence

26 Douglas MacArthur — commander Allied forces South Pacific, World War II

27 Lewis Carroll — author Charles Dodgson Lutwidge; Alice in Wonderland
    Wolfgang Amadeus Mozart — 18th century Austrian composer

29 William McKinley — 25th president, assassinated September 14, 1910
    Thomas Paine — revolutionary leader; *Common Sense*

31 Zane Grey — author of western novels; *Riders of the Purple Sage*
    Jackie Robinson — first African-American man to play professional baseball
    Anna Pavlova — world-famous Russian ballerina

"... that day when all children ... will be able to join hands
and sing ... Free at last! Free at least!"

Martin Luther King, Jr.
I Have a Dream

 TSD 2365-8 *The Elementary Calendar*

Martin Luther King, Jr.

"I have a dream. I have a dream that . . .
little children will one day live in a
nation where they will not be judged by
the color of their skin but by the content
of their character. I have a dream . . ."

Those words were spoken by Dr. Martin Luther King, Jr., in a famous speech he made in Washington, DC, in 1963. Dr. King dreamed that all people could be treated equally and that they could live together in peace.

Martin Luther King, Jr., was born in Atlanta, Georgia, in 1929. He became a Baptist minister and received a doctorate in philosophy. In 1954 he began his first job as a minister in Montgomery, Alabama.

In 1955, Dr. King received a telephone call from the black leaders of the city. They were very angry because a woman named Rosa Parks had been put in jail. She had refused to give up her seat on a city bus to a white man and the bus driver had her arrested. The leaders of the black community wanted to boycott the bus company by asking all black people to stay off the buses. Dr. King became the leader of the boycott and led peaceful demonstrations to show the unfairness of the policies of the bus company and the city. Dr. King was threatened and his home was bombed, but he and the other protestors persisted. In the end, the bus company was defeated. The black people of Montgomery had won; they would be treated fairly on the city buses.

This was just the beginning of what we call the Civil Rights Movement. Soon people all over the country began to protest against unfair laws and the cruel treatment of African Americans in the United States. Dr. King became the best-known leader of this movement. He led marches and made speeches about equal housing, equality in schools, and fair treatment in jobs. He urged action, but he always insisted on action in a peaceful, "nonviolent" manner. Sometimes his followers were put in jail; sometimes they were beaten or bombarded by bottles and stones, but they kept on protesting peacefully.

Very slowly, changes were made affecting the treatment of African Americans. Laws were passed to make changes in housing, to end segregation, and to end discrimination in hiring. In 1964, Dr. King was awarded the Nobel Peace Prize for his work. He was the youngest winner ever.

Many people admired Dr. King for his courage and his ideas, but others hated him and were afraid of the changes he was helping to make. In April 1968, Dr. King went to Memphis, Tennessee, to help organize a march. He was shot and died there. The whole country was shocked and sad.

To show our respect for Dr. King's work and his beliefs, we celebrate his birthday. The third Monday in January has been made a national holiday.

Jack Frost Can Nip and Bite

Winter Safety

❄ Dress in layers of clothing.

❄ Stay dry—change out of wet clothes.

❄ Keep head, hands, and feet warm.

❄ Go indoors for "warm-up" breaks.

If your body becomes too cold, it will draw the heat from the outer parts toward its center. This is why your toes, fingers, ears, and nose feel the cold first.

FROSTNIP happens when skin gets deeply chilled. The skin becomes numb and very pale. Warm the frostnipped part with lukewarm (not hot) water or tuck it against a warm body area. A tingling feeling will tell you that the frostnipped part is returning to normal.

FROSTBITE is much more serious than frostnip. The skin becomes blotchy or spotted and turns to a grayish-yellow, and then to a grayish-blue. The skin is not just numb, it is frozen.

A frostbitten area must be warmed slowly and carefully to prevent tissue damage. Warm (not hot) water works best.

DO NOT:

❄ Rub the frozen part to warm it.

❄ Use water that is too warm.

❄ Try to warm the part near a fire.

A person with frostbite **must** see a **doctor**!

Staying Warm (and Dry) from Head to Toe

A lot of body heat is lost through the head. Cover your head and ears with a warm hat.

A scarf keeps cold air from sneaking in around your neck and under your collar.

Wear layers of clothing: long underwear, one or two thin wool sweaters, and a windproof jacket with tightly fitted cuffs. Air warmed by your body will be trapped between the layers of clothing inside your jacket.

That is how animals keep warm in the winter. Fluffy feathers or fur traps and holds body heat in the air around the animals' bodies.

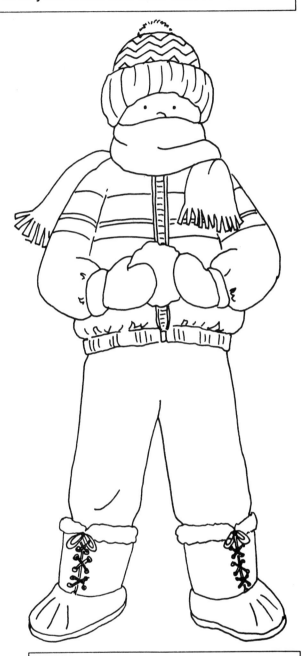

Mittens are warmer than gloves. Why? Because they trap the warm air around your fingers. Gloves do not leave enough air space.

Everybody likes to wear jeans, but denim is not at all warm. When denim becomes wet, it can be as cold and stiff as a popsicle! Wear wool, woolblends, or corduroy pants.

Layer your feet, too. Wear thin nylon or woolblend socks under another pair of wool socks. Rubber boots help keep out the cold and wet.

If you get *too* warm you can take something off. Sweating, just like getting wet, causes rapid heat loss.

TSD 2365-8 *The Elementary Calendar*

School Nurse's Day
Your School Nurse . . .

. . . keeps records of your height, weight, allergies, and other special problems.

. . . checks your eyes and ears

. . . helps with school dental checkups and trips to the dentist.

. . . gives first aid for bumps, bruises, cuts, scrapes, and broken bones.

. . . assists the school doctor with examinations.

. . . works with the administration on good student attendance.

. . . likes children.

. . .dispenses medicine your doctor wants you to take.

. . . wants you to stay healthy and safe.

. . . protects the health of your teachers, too.

Draw a picture of your school nurse or a picture of something he or she does.

. . . teaches about the family, drug and alcohol abuse, nutrition, and hygiene.

. . . sends letters home about strep throat, chicken pox, and other diseases you might catch.

. . . must have nurses' training, a bachelor's degree, and a health education certificate.

To make a card, cut out the picture and mount on a folded piece of 6" x 9" (152 x 229 mm) construction paper.

The Chinese New Year

The Chinese New Year begins on the first day of the first month of the lunar (moon) calendar—between late January and mid-February on the Gregorian (solar) calendar and lasts for fifteen days.

Preparations for this important event begin sixteen days before it, when businesspeople settle their accounts and give thanks if they have had a good year. Four days later it is time to "sweep floors clean." Both men and women help with the housecleaning. About a week before the big celebration, Zao Wang, the kitchen god whose picture hangs in every kitchen, goes to heaven to report on the family's behavior during the year. To prepare him for the journey he is offered chicken, duck, and fish. His lips are rubbed with honey so that he will say only sweet things about the family. After prayers, his picture is wrapped in a paper chariot and set afire to sent him on his way. On New Year's Day a new picture of Zao Wang is hung in the kitchen.

Special foods are prepared for the holiday: melon seeds, preserved fruit, fried sesame seed cakes, peanuts, and molasses are just some of them. Knives cannot be used to cut food because all sharp objects are hidden. They might cut off one's luck!

On New Year's Eve, people go into the streets to welcome the New Year. They believe this will give them long life. On New Year's Day children *kowtow* (bow) to their parents to show respect. Families hang red scrolls printed with wishes for good luck in their homes and children are given coins in little red packets. Everywhere, people wish one another good fortune for the coming year.

A huge dragon, a Chinese symbol of good luck, leads the New Year's procession. It is made of bamboo covered with paper or silk. Fifty people might be needed to hold it up as it weaves and winds through the streets. Dancers, acrobats, clowns, and stiltwalkers accompany the dragon while firecrackers pop and crackle to scare away evil spirits.

The long, exciting holiday ends with the Lantern Festival. Torches are lighted to help people see heavenly spirits as they fly across the first full moon of the year. Children light candles inside lanterns of many shapes and carry them through the streets. Older children carry long bamboo torches. With the New Year made welcome, everyone returns home to enjoy the good fortune it is sure to bring and to wait for the next year's wonderful celebration.

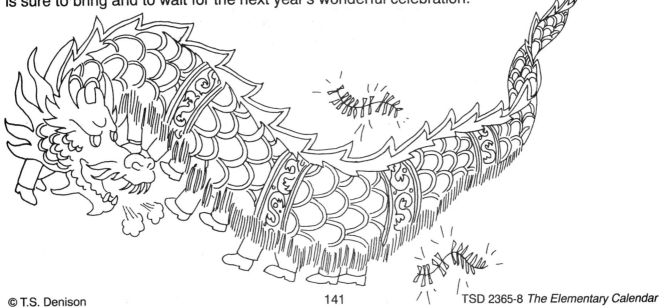

Chinese New Year Dragon

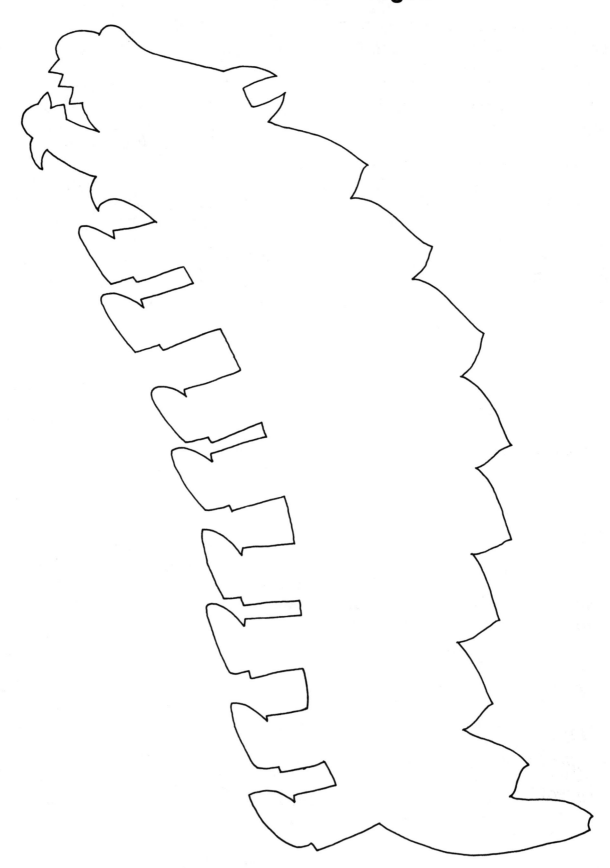

Feasts for Feathered Friends

1. Wind a string into the top of a pinecone; make it long enough to tie to a branch. Push and poke peanut butter into all the spaces of the cone. You can roll the peanut butter pinecone in birdseed before you hang it.

   Variation: Punch a hole in the edge of a plastic lid, poke the string through it, and fill the lid with peanut butter.

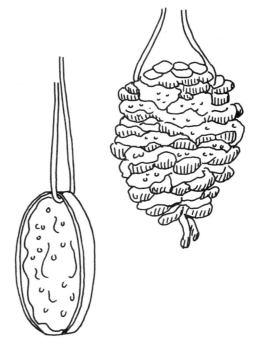

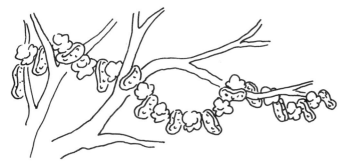

2. Use a needle and heavy thread to string popcorn and unsalted peanuts (in the shell). Hang over the branches of a tree.

3. Orange peels or pieces of apple make a special treat for birds.

   And do not forget that sandwich crust you did not eat!

4. Buy a piece of suet from the supermarket or the butcher. Tie or hang it in a tree. Press it into some birdseed.

Can you name these feathered friends?

bluejay, cardinal, chickadee

"Signs" of Winter

Front

Back

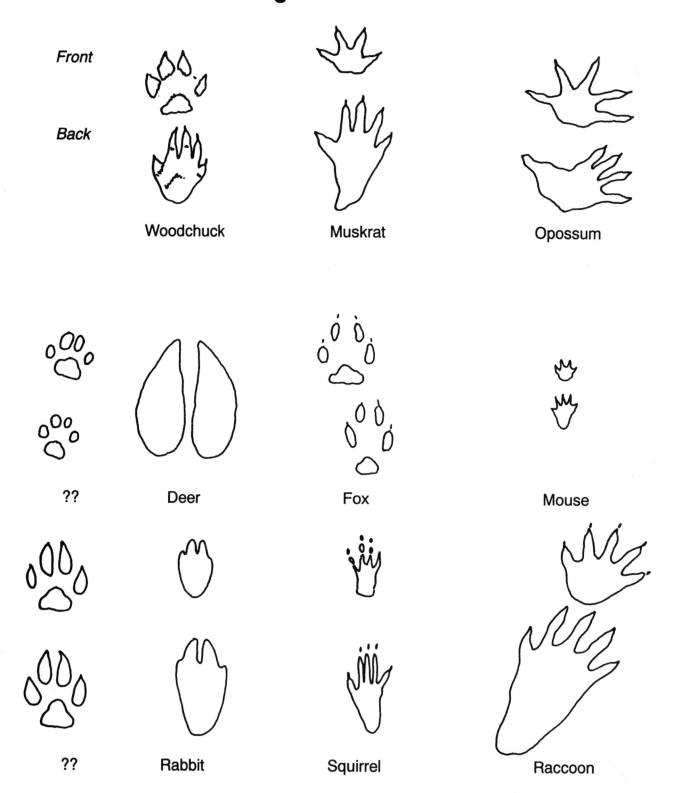

Woodchuck

Muskrat

Opossum

??

Deer

Fox

Mouse

??

Rabbit

Squirrel

Raccoon

Make "tracks" outdoors and be a winter detective!

You may find some of these tracks right in your own backyard. The two sets of tracks without names are easy to find and identify. What are they?

Mitten Matching

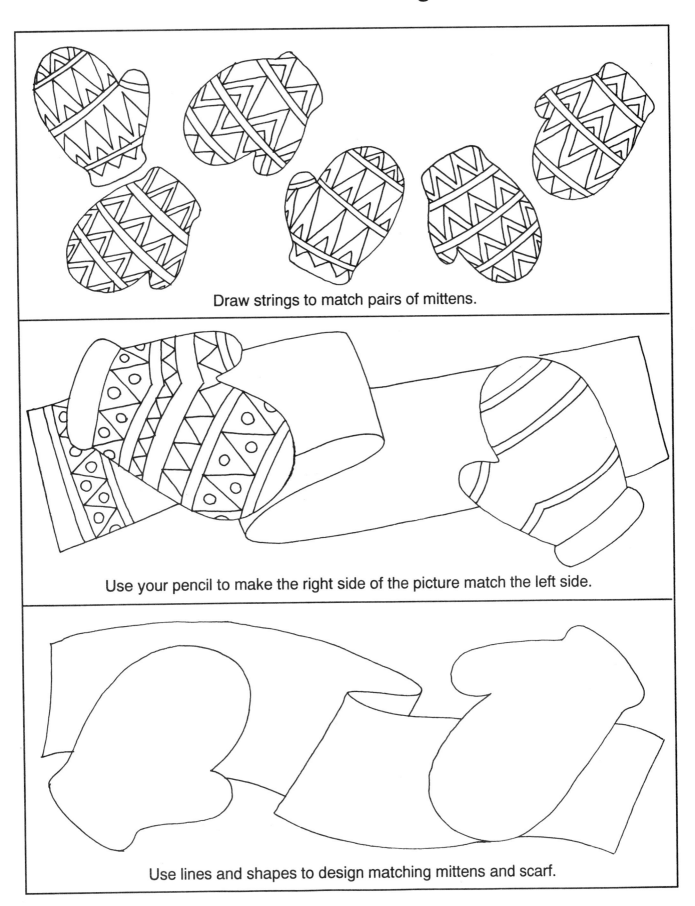

Draw strings to match pairs of mittens.

Use your pencil to make the right side of the picture match the left side.

Use lines and shapes to design matching mittens and scarf.

TSD 2365-8 *The Elementary Calendar*

Make a Snowflake

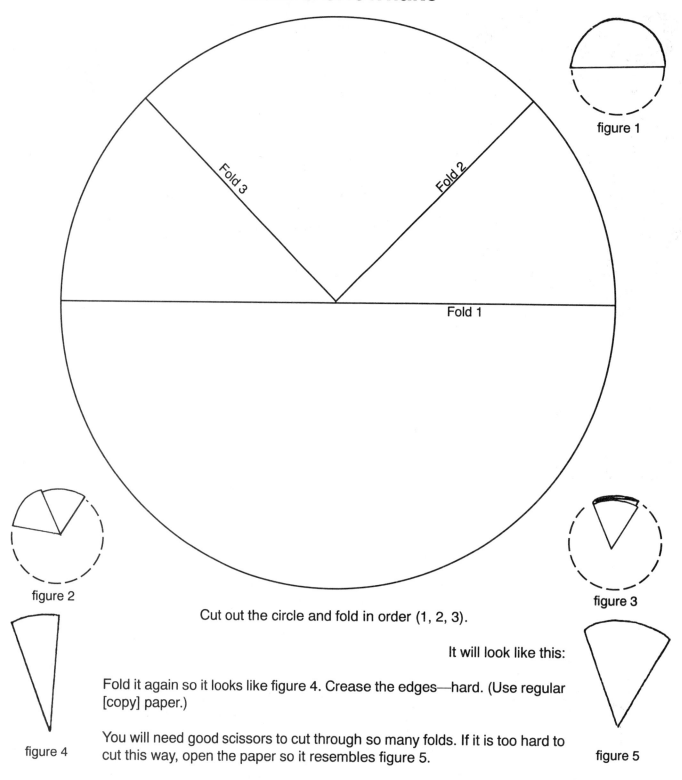

figure 1

Fold 3

Fold 2

Fold 1

figure 2

figure 3

Cut out the circle and fold in order (1, 2, 3).

It will look like this:

Fold it again so it looks like figure 4. Crease the edges—hard. (Use regular [copy] paper.)

You will need good scissors to cut through so many folds. If it is too hard to cut this way, open the paper so it resembles figure 5.

figure 4

figure 5

Either way, make lots of snips from each edge (but not all the way across). Your lacy snowflake should have six points. Make many of them in different sizes. Hang them everywhere!

TSD 2365-8 *The Elementary Calendar*

You really "WRAPPED UP" all your work today!

A Gold Seal for GREAT WORK!

AWARD

AN

No "HOME"WORK for TODAY!

is STARTING THE NEW YEAR RIGHT!

TSD 2365-8 *The Elementary Calendar*

Word Search

```
        F B N C D
  E J F G F R E E Z E H
  I A J K I O L W M N O
  W I N T E R S P Y Q M R
  S T U I V E T W E X I Y
  Z A A M B P C D A E T F
  G H R E I L J K R L T M
  B A B Y N H A T S A B E C F
  N O P S Q R C O L D S N T U
  I V S K A T E W E X Y S Z A
  C B N I C S D E D F G H I
  E J O K L C I C I C L E M
  N Q W P R A H O C K E Y S
  T U V W R Y X Z A C F
        G H F I R S T I
```

Find and circle these words:

SNOW	JANUARY	WINTER	FIRST
COLD	ICICLE	BABY	SCARF
ICE	FIREPLACE	NEW YEAR	FREEZE
SKATE	SKI	TIME	MITTENS
SLED	HOCKEY	HAT	FROST

Name _____

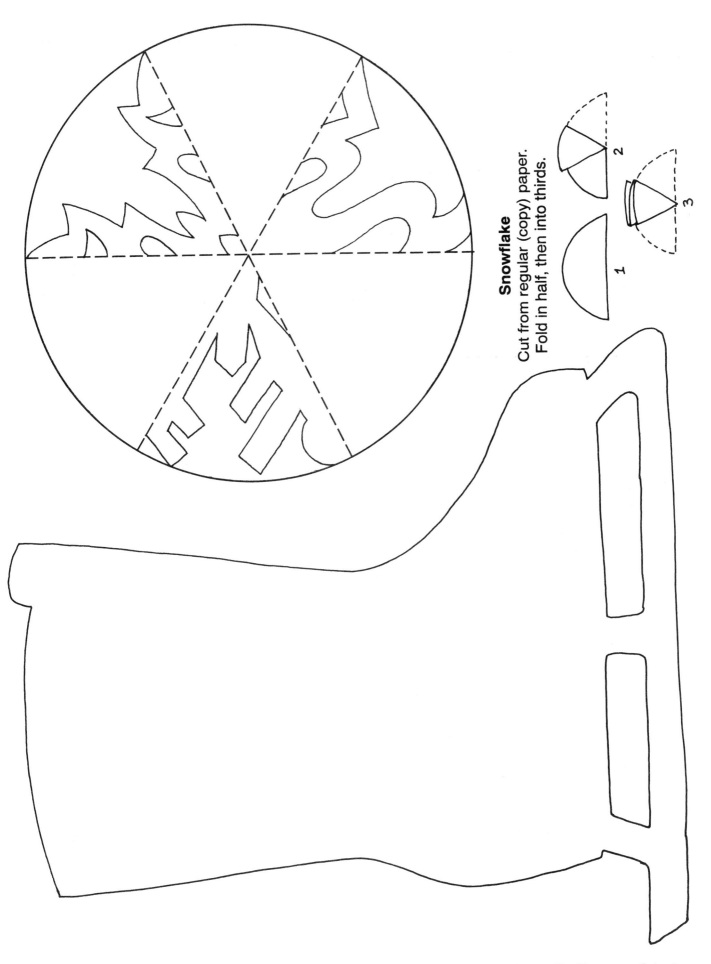

Snowflake

Cut from regular (copy) paper.
Fold in half, then into thirds.

1

2

3

Snowflakes

Materials: copy paper

Cut circle from paper. Fold in half, then in thirds as shown. If paper thickness allows, fold again. Cut design leaving enough of the folded edges intact so that the snowflake holds together, but cut well into the triangular base. Completely cut away rounded edge. Practice using curved lines, angular lines, and combinations.

Away with four-pointed and round snowflakes!

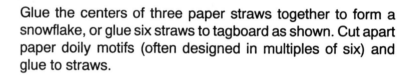

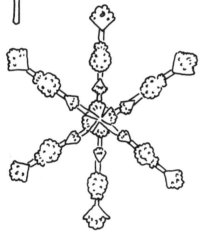

Straw Snowflakes

Materials: paper straws, doilies

Glue the centers of three paper straws together to form a snowflake, or glue six straws to tagboard as shown. Cut apart paper doily motifs (often designed in multiples of six) and glue to straws.

Watch the placement! Glue one section to each straw before adding a second motif. This will keep them nearly identical.

If using six straws, cover tagboard base with central motif.

If time and patience permit, both sides may be covered and snowflakes hung to turn freely.

Scarf and Mittens

Materials: yarn

Precut colored paper into 6" x 18" (152 x 457 mm) and 4½" x 6" (115 x 152 mm) sizes. Provide a mitten pattern to fit smaller paper.

Have children select two of the smaller papers in the same color and one of the larger to match or contrast. Trace mitten pattern on one of the small papers, hold both together and cut out mittens. Use crayons or markers to make simple repeat designs, matching mittens and scarf. Fringe ends of scarf.

Staple mittens to ends of yarn and then to scarf with yarn, or omit yarn and glue or staple directly to scarf.

TSD 2365-8 *The Elementary Calendar*

A Trip to the Tropics!

Use crayons or markers to help this flower grow—one ring at a time.
(*Hint:* some letters make great designs!)
We have started the flower for you. Keep it growing!
For more fun: Make some green leaves and glue them to the back of the flower.

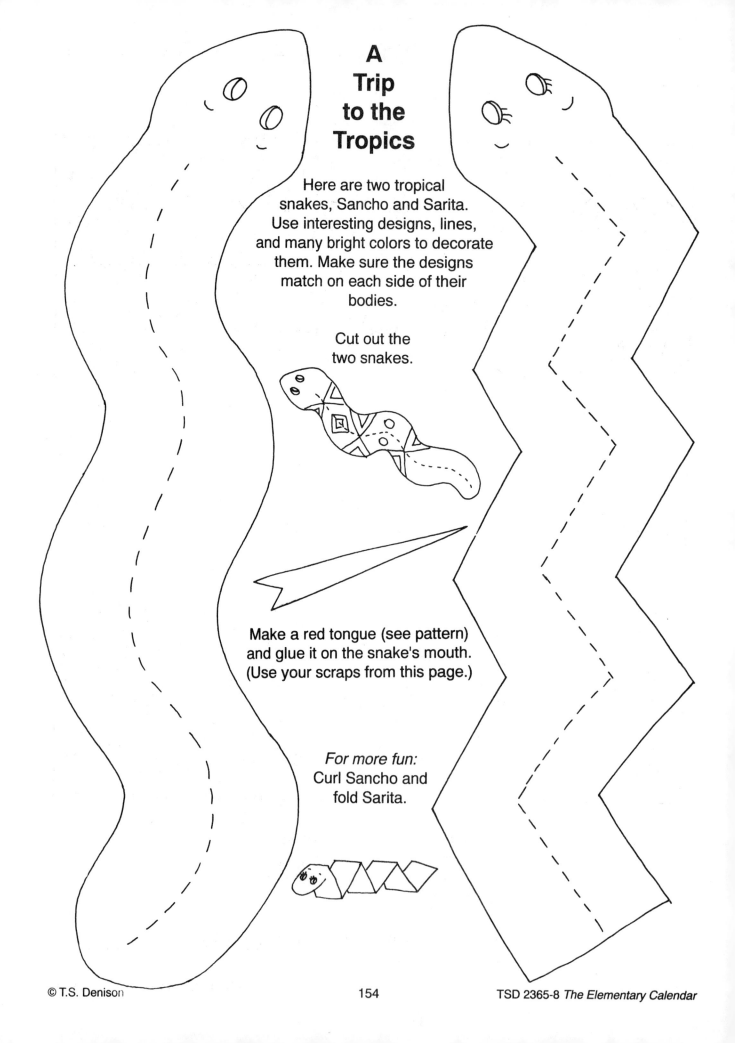

A Trip to the Tropics

Here are two tropical snakes, Sancho and Sarita. Use interesting designs, lines, and many bright colors to decorate them. Make sure the designs match on each side of their bodies.

Cut out the two snakes.

Make a red tongue (see pattern) and glue it on the snake's mouth. (Use your scraps from this page.)

For more fun: Curl Sancho and fold Sarita.

TSD 2365-8 *The Elementary Calendar*

Name _____

1 – red   5 – green
2 – yellow   6 – purple
3 – blue   7 – light purple
4 – orange

Color the confetti and bubbles in many bright colors.

February Contents

BECAUSE YOU'RE

"FIRST" WITH US!

Sunday	Monday	Tuesday	Wednesday	Thursday	Friday	Saturday

February

3	Norman Rockwell	illustrator of American life
	Elizabeth Blackwell	first female physician in the United States; abolitionist; feminist
	Income Tax	16th Amendment ratified, 1913
4	Boy Scouts of America	founded 1910
	Charles Lindbergh	American aviator, first person to fly solo across the Atlantic, 1927
6	Ronald Reagan	40th president
	Babe Ruth	baseball hero, nicknamed the "Sultan of Swat"
7	Charles Dickens	English novelist, social critic; *Oliver Twist*
8	Jules Verne	"Father of science fiction"; *Twenty Thousand Leagues Under the Sea*
9	William Henry Harrison	9th president; died of pneumonia after only thirty-two days in office
11	Thomas Edison	American inventor; over 1,000 patents
12	Abraham Lincoln	16th president; ended slavery; assassinated April 14, 1865
	Charles Darwin	English naturalist; pioneered theory of evolution
15	Susan B. Anthony	reformer; feminist leader
22	George Washington	first president; revolutionary hero
	Robert Baden-Powell	founder of Boy Scout and Girl Guide movement
26	William Cody	"Buffalo Bill," frontiersman; showman
	Grand Canyon	became a National Park, 1919
	Levi Strauss	made first jeans for California gold miners
27	Henry Wadsworth Longfellow	poet and writer; "Paul Revere's Ride"

Groundhog Day

Legend says that if the groundhog wakes up from
his winter's sleep and sees his shadow,
there will be six more weeks of winter.

Inventor's Day

made by: _____ ®

The _____ Machine

Professor I.M. Smart forgot to finish his invention.
It is up to you. Use your imagination and draw many parts to finish his machine.

Now give it a name.

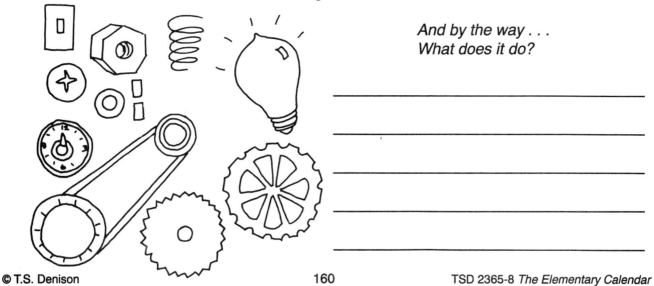

And by the way . . .
What does it do?

_____

_____

_____

_____

_____

Inventor's Day—Birthday of Thomas Edison

Thomas Alva Edison was probably America's greatest inventor. His more famous inventions were: the phonograph, the incandescent light bulb, the movie projector, and the alkaline storage battery. Edison also helped with or improved many other inventions including the typewriter, the telegraph, and the telephone. Thomas Edison opened the door for modern electronics when he discovered how to control the flow of electrical current.

Today, whenever we use any of our modern appliances, when we watch a movie or listen to music, when we send a telegram, make a telephone call, and when we ride in a car, we can say "Thank you" to Thomas Alva Edison.

SOME EDISON FACTS

Thomas Edison held over 1,000 patents; over 300 were for electric light, heat, and power.

The phonograph was Edison's favorite invention because it brought music into every home. Edison believed that "music, next to religion, had done more (for) man than any other thing . . ."

Although Edison invented the phonograph for our listening pleasure, he himself was deaf. He "listened" to recordings by biting the wood frame of the phonograph so that vibrations traveled through his teeth and jaw into his inner ear.

Edison believed that his deafness, because it shut out all disturbing noises while he slept, allowed him to get four hours of rest in fifteen minutes of sleep. He slept, therefore, very little, preferring to "catnap" for a few minutes at a time in his laboratory.

It took five years and 50,000 experiments to complete the storage battery to Edison's satisfaction. (A storage battery "holds" energy for use in cars, portable radios, flashlights, etc.)

The underground electric cables installed at Edison's winter home in Fort Myers, Florida, in 1885 are still in use today. A light bulb in his laboratory still burns.

It was Edison who said, "Genius is one per cent inspiration and ninety-nine per cent perspiration."

And guess who invented the first talking doll . . . before 1900?!

Name _____

Dental Health Month

Take your own dental survey!

Answer the questions below. For some of them you will need help from Mom and Dad. When you have the answers, compare them with your classmates' answers and fill in your Dental Survey. Use the answer you received *most* often for the survey questions.

Questions

_____ 1. How old were you when you got your first tooth?

_____ 2. What kind of tooth was it? Top, bottom, back, front?

_____ 3. How old were you when you lost your first tooth? (If you have not lost a tooth, ask an older friend who has.)

_____ 4. How many teeth do you have altogether (including *waiting* spaces)?

_____ 5. How many teeth do grown-ups have?

Your Dental Survey

_____ 1. Most children get their first teeth when they are about _____.

_____ 2. The _____ teeth are usually the first to come in.

_____ 3. Most children begin losing their first (baby) teeth when they are _____ years old.

_____ 4. Most children have _____ (how many) baby teeth?

_____ 5. Grown-ups have _____ (how many) teeth?

Dental Health Month

Fill in any blanks in the sentences below, then match the numbers and place those words into the puzzle. Also, add the bold faced words to the puzzle. The letters in the darker squares will spell two important words.

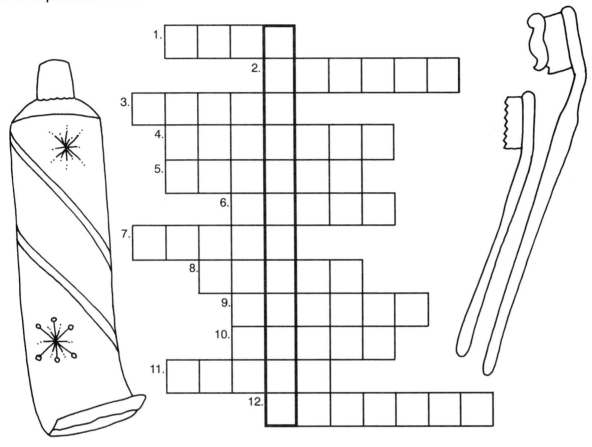

1. Our teeth help us to chew our _____.

2. Our teeth are covered with **ENAMEL**. It is harder than bone.

3. The **CROWN** is the part of a tooth that shows above the gum.

4. See your _____ for regular dental checkups.

5. Our back teeth, called **MOLARS**, help to grind our food.

6. Brush and floss to keep your teeth _____.

7. _____ after meals and at bedtime.

8. Take care of your _____. They are important to you.

9. A **CAVITY** is a hole in the enamel of your tooth.

10. Clean between your teeth with dental _____.

11. The **ROOTS** of your teeth hold them in place in your jaw bones.

12. Good dental **HYGIENE** will keep your teeth clean and healthy.

Once there was a handsome tooth,
Quite Proud of his shine and style,
And especially of the part
he helped to play in a smile.

The Truth
About A Tooth

But he really went too far!!

fold

Then one day he said to the toothbrush,
the floss, and good foods, too,

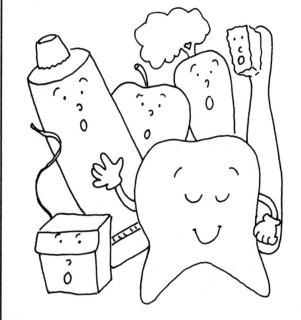

"Good-by old friends, I don't need you!
I'm off to try something new!"

fold

So he chewed some of this . . .

And a small bite of that . . .

For Healthy Teeth . . .

Do not forget who your real friends are!

Africa Word Search

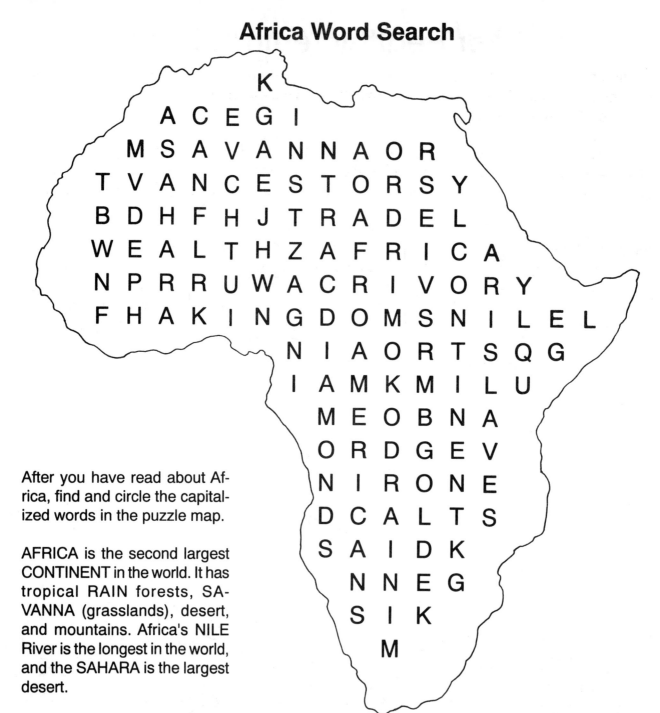

```
            K
      A C E G I
    M S A V A N N A O R
    T V A N C E S T O R S Y
    B D H F H J T R A D E L
    W E A L T H Z A F R I C A
    N P R R U W A C R I V O R Y
    F H A K I N G D O M S N I L E L
          N I A O R T S Q G
          I A M K M I L U
          M E O B N A
          O R D G E V
          N I R O N E
          D C A L T S
          S A I D K
          N N E G
          S I K
          M
```

After you have read about Africa, find and circle the capitalized words in the puzzle map.

AFRICA is the second largest CONTINENT in the world. It has tropical RAIN forests, SAVANNA (grasslands), desert, and mountains. Africa's NILE River is the longest in the world, and the SAHARA is the largest desert.

Because Africa is almost completely surrounded by water, many ships went there to TRADE. European traders were amazed at the WEALTH of the ancient African KINGDOMS. They were rich in GOLD, IRON, IVORY, and DIAMONDS. When the New World was being settled and workers were needed to farm the land, a cruel new trade began—in African SLAVES. Millions of Africans from many different tribes were shipped to America and forced to work the land. Many of these slaves were the ANCESTORS of today's African Americans.

Today, people of African descent live all over the world. Although they are from many different tribal groups, all of them may share in the rich and colorful history of Africa.

A Time Line of African-American History

A time line can be as simple or as elaborate as you choose to make it. It might consist of significant historical events; African-American "firsts"; Civil Rights milestones; achievements in various areas; or a combination of any of these.

A long hallway is best for the presentation of the line to give some idea of the period of years of African American history. Because events often cluster in certain periods, exact measurement or strict division into years does not work well. Spacing of information along the line is a matter of judgement.

To construct the time line:
- Cut black paper to make a line six inches wide on the wall
- Attach significant dates along the line using 6" x 9" (152 x 229 mm) white paper
- Above and below the line place 4½" x 6" (115 x 152 mm) cards (with arrows where necessary), color coded for history, science, Civil Rights, etc., if you like.

To make the work easier, divide it among several classes.

To store: clip events to appropriate years and file.

The lists of dates, events, and facts on the following pages are given to save time in research. Add important facts of your own or select only the information you need for your particular time line.

African-American History Time Line

1619   Dutch ship delivers twenty black indentured servants to Jamestown.

1624   Slavery spreads northward to New England and Fugitive Slave Laws are passed to deal with runaways.

1688   First formal protest against slavery by Pennsylvania Quakers

1700   About 28,000 slaves in North America with almost 23,000 of them in the South

1750   Crispus Attucks escapes from his master in Massachusetts.
Slave population reaches 236,400 (20% of the total colonial population).

1770   Crispus Attucks is one of the first men killed in Boston Massacre

1775–1783   8,000–10,000 black soldiers fight bravely in Revolution, although *free versus slave* still is an issue.

1777   Vermont becomes first state to abolish slavery.

1783   Massachusetts outlaws slavery.

1790   757,000 African-Americans in United States, 9% are free

1793   Cotton gin strengthens slavery as more workers are needed

1808   1,000,000 slaves are in United States; federal law bans further import.

1812   Commander Oliver Hazard Perry praises the African Americans on his ship in the War of 1812 (Blacks account for one-sixth of the naval force)

1820   Missouri Compromise bans slavery north of Missouri making twelve slave states and twelve free states

1827   New York abolishes slavery, frees 10,000 African Americans

1831   Nat Turner leads largest United States slave rebellion in Virginia

1843   Sojourner Truth begins work as abolitionist

1847   Frederick Douglass, antislavery lecturer, publishes the *North Star*

1849   Harriet Tubman escapes from slavery and returns south nineteen times to free 300 slaves through "underground railroad."

1852   *Uncle Tom's Cabin* by Harriet Beecher Stowe published

1857   Dred Scott Decision opens United States territories to slavery, denies rights of black citizens

1858   Lincoln-Douglas Debates
1859   Abolitionist John Brown attacks federal arsenal at Harpers Ferry.

1860 Lincoln is elected president.
      South Carolina secedes from the Union.

1861 Civil War begins with attack on Fort Sumter

1863 Lincoln signs Emancipation Proclamation

1865 Confederate Army accepts black soldiers, but too late to help the South.
      Lee surrenders at Appamattox, Virginia; Civil War ends.
      Thirteenth Amendment abolishes slavery.
      Lincoln is assassinated
      186,000 African Americans served in Union army, 38,000 killed in battle, 126,000 dead
      from disease

1868 Fourteenth Amendment—"All citizens" given protection under Constitution

1870 Fifteenth Amendment—guarantees "all citizens" right to vote.

1875 Civil Rights Act bans discrimination in public places.

1896 *Plessy v. Ferguson* decision leads to "separate but equal" segregation.

1909 NAACP (National Association for the Advancement of Colored People) founded on Lincoln's
      (100th) birthday

1915 2,000,000 blacks migrate to northern industrial centers.

1917 World War I—over 300,000 African Americans will serve, 1400 as commissioned officers.
      11% of overseas troops are black; first French crosses are awarded to blacks.

1919 83 recorded lynchings; 200 public Klan meetings; 25 major race riots

1923 500,000 blacks leave the South.

1924 Immigration law bars African blacks from United States.

1926 Negro History Week introduced

1936 Jesse Owens wins four Olympic gold medals in Berlin; this embarrasses Hitler.

1940 Benjamin O. Davis, Sr., becomes first black United States general

1941 United States enters World War II
      More than 1 million African-American men and women will serve before war ends in 1945.

1947 Truman's Committee on Civil Rights condemns racial injustice

1954 Supreme Court finds "separate but equal" unconstitutional in *Brown v. Board of Education
      of Topeka*, and outlaws segregation in public education

1955 Rosa Parks refuses to surrender bus seat to a white man. Bus boycott begins under direc-
      tion of Reverend Martin Luther King, Jr., in Montgomery, Alabama.

1960	Period of Civil Rights activism begins with student "sit-ins" in the south
1962	James Meredith enters University of Mississippi protected by 12,000 troops
1963	250,000 people march on Washington; Dr. Martin Luther King, Jr., gives "I Have a Dream..." speech Civil Rights leader Medgar Evers is assassinated in Jackson, Mississippi.
1963	President John F. Kennedy assassinated
1964	Major Civil Rights bill passed under President Lyndon B. Johnson Reverend Martin Luther King, Jr., wins the Nobel Peace Prize.
1965	Selma to Montgomery March led by Dr. King Malcom X shot and killed in New York Watts riots in Los Angeles, 3,598 arrested, damages of over $46 million
1965–1970	Turbulent period of Civil Rights gains and losses Protests, sit-ins, marches, and riots in major cities
1968	King's assassination triggers violence in over one hundred cities Robert Kennedy assassinated in Los Angeles
1970–1975	School segregation continues even in the north Black Civil Rights groups split into radicals and conservatives
1977	Alex Haley's Roots wins the Pulitzer Prize
1980s	Saint Louis schools finally desegregate twenty-six years after court order African-Americans make gains in elections Battles over housing discrimination and other areas continue Aparteid in South Africa becomes an issue Jesse Jackson runs for President

Two More Activities for African-American History Month

A Legacy
Collect pictures or posters (or make collages) of African Americans from various areas of achievement. Surround each with "fact cards" regarding previous achievements in the same area.
For example: Post pictures of Oprah Winfrey, Colin Powell, Kirby Puckett, etc., surrounded by "firsts" and records of other famous African-American role models.

Diversity and Unity
Unless you are a Native American, your roots lie in another country. As Americans, we must all live together peacably.

Use a large world map or make a chart to show various countries. Around it, or on it, place cards with students' names and one or two lines to show their origins. (Draw the lines or use yarn which can be moved as you go along.)

Black Firsts in the United States

First African American . . .

1624	William Tucker	child born in American colonies
1783	James Derham	physician in United States
1785	John Morront	missionary minister to work with Native Americans
1826	John Russwurm	college graduate (Bowdoin College, Maine
	Edward A. Jones	may have graduated days earlier (Amherst)
1834	Henry Blair	to obtain patent (corn-planting machine)
1845	Macon B. Allen	formally admitted to bar (Massachusetts)
1853	William Wells Brown	published work (*Clotel, or the President's Daughter*)
1862	Mary Jane Patterson	woman to graduate from college (Oberlin)
1865	Martin R. Delany	to achieve military rank of major
	John Rock	admitted to practice before U.S. Supreme Court
1866	Charles L. Mitchell	elected to a northern state legislature (Massachusetts)
1870	Richard T. Greener	to receive degree from Harvard
	Jonathan Jasper Wright	elected to State Supreme Court (South Carolina)
1872	Charlotte E. Roy	woman to graduate from law school (Howard University)
	Dr. Rebecca J. Cole	woman physician (Female Medical College of Pennsylvania)
1875	Oscar Lewis	jockey to win the first Kentucky Derby
1879	Mary E. Mattoney	woman to receive nursing diploma
1882	W.S. Scott	daily newspaper owner (The *Cairo Illinois Gazette*)
1884	Moses Fleetwood Walker	major league baseball player (Toledo)
1885	Cuban Giants	professional baseball team (New York City)
1890	Thomy Gafon	millionaire (Louisiana)
1903	Maggie Walker	woman bank president (Virginia)
1907	Alain Leroy Locke	Rhodes Scholar
1908	Alpha Kappa Alpha	sorority founded (Howard University)
1916	"Fritz" Pollard	all-American football player (Brown University) to play pro-football for major team (1919)
1923	Renaissance	basketball team organized
1926	Violette Anderson	woman lawyer—United States Supreme Court
1938	Crystal Bird Fauset	woman elected to state legislature (Pennsylvania)
1939	Jane Matilda Bolin	woman judge (New York City)
1940	Hattie McDaniel	to win Oscar (*Gone With the Wind*)
	Benjamin O. Davis, Sr.	brigadier general in United States
	Booker T. Washington	honored on United States postage stamp

First African American . . .

1942	Bernard W. Robinson	commissioned naval officer
1943	W.E.B. Dubois	admitted to National Institute of Arts and Letters
1944	Harry S. McAlpin	accredited White House news correspondent
1946	Roy Campanella	to manage baseball team on the field
1947	Dan Bankhead	pitcher in major leagues, Leroy Satchel Paige follows in 1948
1949	Jackie Robinson	to win league's Most Valuable Player award
1950	Ralph Bunche	to receive Nobel Peace Prize
	Arthur Dorrington	to play in professional hockey
1951	William L. Rowe	deputy police commissioner (New York City)
	Janet Collins	principal dancer at the Metropolitan Opera House
1954	National Negro Network	radio network, WOV, New York
1954	Ruth Carol Taylor	airline stewardess
1958	Gloria Davy	to sing at Metropolitan Opera House (in *Aida*)
1961	James Benton Parsons	appointed district court judge
1962	Lieutenant Commander Samuel L. Gravely, Jr.	warship commander (*USS Falgout*)
1966	Emmett Ashford	umpire
	Bill Russell	to direct major league sports team
1967	Thurgood Marshall	appointed to the United States Supreme Court
1968	Henry Lewis	named director of an American orchestra
	Martin Briscoe	quarterback in professional football
1970	Chris Dickerson	to win "Mr. America" title
1977	Karen Farmer	member of the Daughters of the American Revolution
1979	John Glover	Federal Bureau of Investigations field office chief
	Second Lieutenant Marcella A. Hayes	woman pilot in United States armed forces
	Audrey Neal	first woman of any race to be a longshoreman
1981	Pamela Johnson	publisher of major newspaper in the United States (*Ithaca Journal*)
1983	Vanessa Williams	Miss America
	Suzette Charles	runner-up to Vanessa Williams; Miss New Jersey
1986	Lieutenant Commander Donnie Cochran	pilot to fly with navy's elite Blue Angels
1988	Eugene Antonio Marino	Roman Catholic archbishop (Atlanta)
	Lee Roy Young	Texas Ranger
1989	Bill White	president of professional sports league (National League)

African Americans in Sports

Willie Mays

Zina Garrison

Jesse Owens

Earvin "Magic" Johnson

Muhammad Ali

Walter Payton

African Americans in the Performing Arts

Arthur
Mitchell

Louis
"Satchmo"
Armstrong

Lena
Horne

Leontyne
Price

Ray
Charles

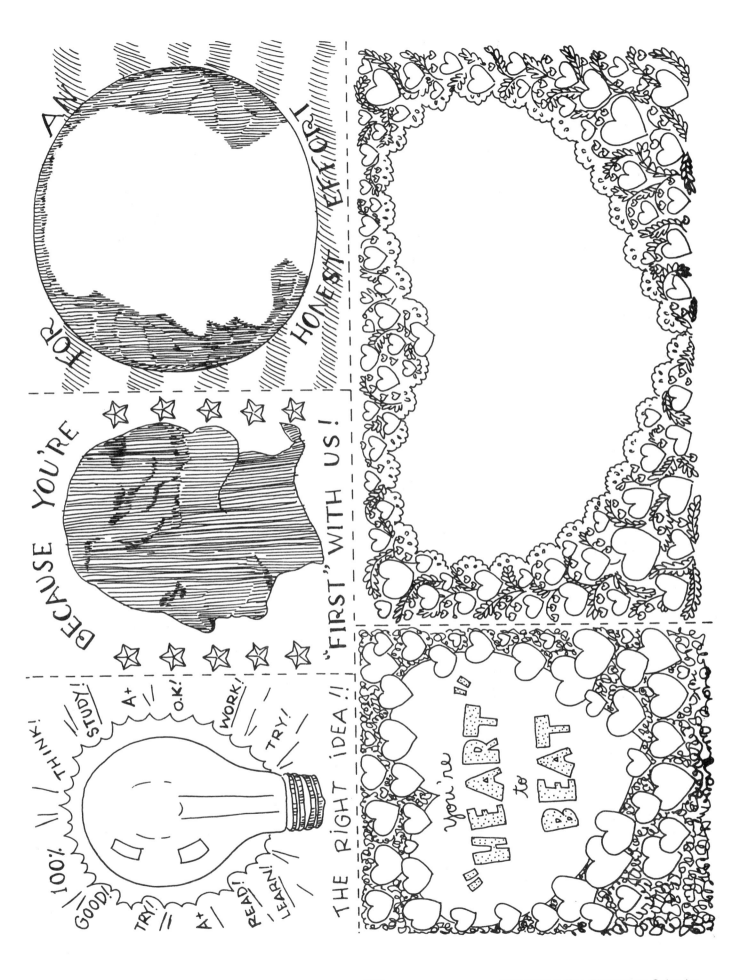

I AM "FIRST" FOR HONEST EFFORT!

BECAUSE YOU'RE "FIRST", WITH US!

100%! THINK! STUDY! A+ O.K. WORK! TRY! GOOD! TRY! A+ READ! LEARN! THE RIGHT IDEA!!

you're "HEART to BEAT"

TSD 2365-8 *The Elementary Calendar*

```
            B A X C O
H W I J I   E F R E D R Z
K L A C E L M   N O P R P Q I J L
C R S U V B O O K S W O R X B H A
I U C H E R R I E S H Y W E Z B O C
A P L I N C O L N V A C D S E O N D
F I G N H I K M O P D Q R I S N E G
L D T G R O U N D H O G U D V S S
I W X T Y Z A C F I W J H E A R T
L M O L N O R Q F R I E N D U
V N O X Z A C D F H J T K L
M O V A L E N T I N E P Q F
R E B I R T H D A Y T U
V W A Y Z A C D F D
    G C A N D Y I
      C H I J
```

VALENTINE	BOOKS	SHADOW	PRESIDENT
HEART	HONEST	LOVE	WASHINGTON
LACE	CHERRIES	RIBBONS	BIRTHDAY
FRIEND	ARROW	LINCOLN	GROUNDHOG
CANDY	RED	CUPID	

Name _____

George Washington

TSD 2365-8 *The Elementary Calendar*

Cherries

Abraham Lincoln

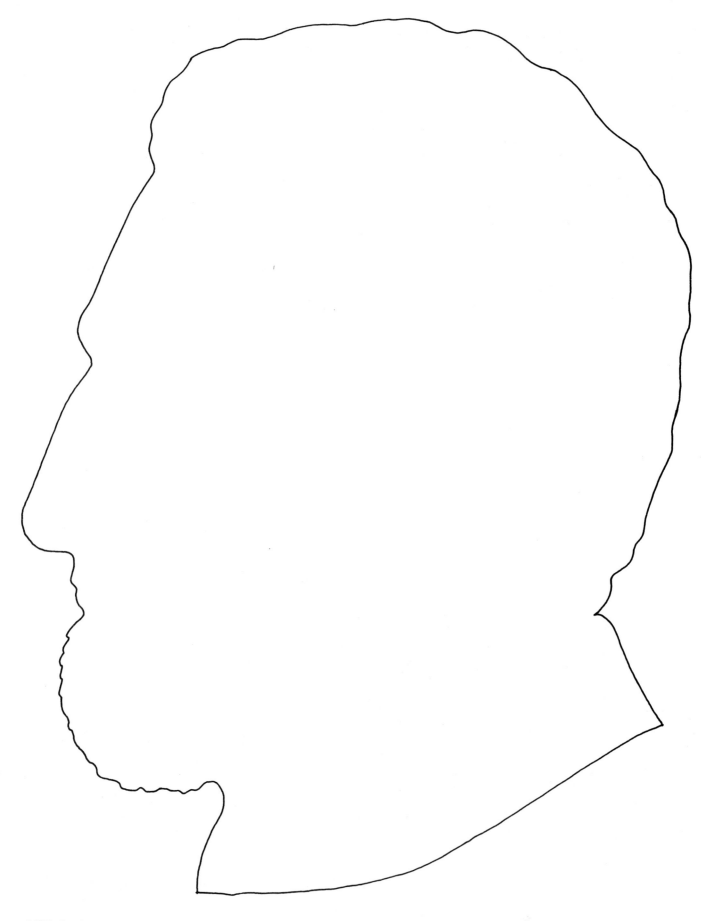

TSD 2365-8 *The Elementary Calendar*

Stovepipe hat

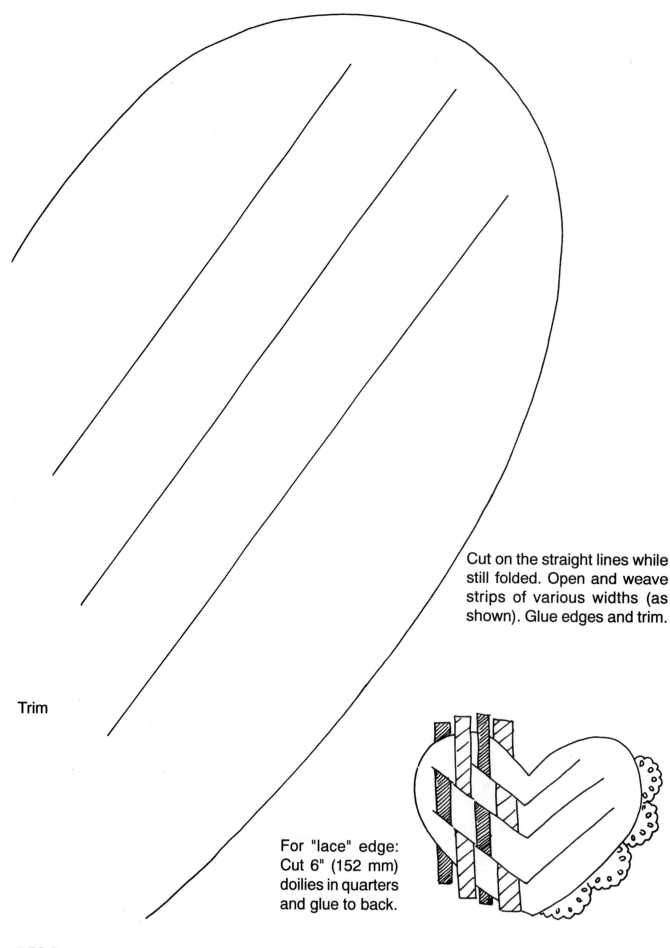

Cut on the straight lines while still folded. Open and weave strips of various widths (as shown). Glue edges and trim.

Trim

For "lace" edge: Cut 6" (152 mm) doilies in quarters and glue to back.

TSD 2365-8 *The Elementary Calendar*

Simple Frame

Materials: 12" (305 mm) square white and other colors of paper

Hold squares of paper together with white on the top and fold the corners (both sheets at once) to the center. Fold center points back to center of sides and staple. Fill the center of the frame with drawing, mosaic, or paper sculpture.

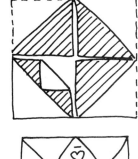
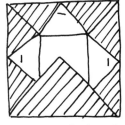

Valentine Animals

Materials: doilies, red and pink paper, heart patterns in various sizes

Make the lion, mouse, lamb, and other animals using whole and half-heart shapes. (Doilies separate more easily from the middle than from the edges.) Rub firmly between thumb and fingers.

Woven Valentines

Materials: 9" (229 mm) or 12" (305 mm) strips in a variety of widths and valentine colors, 9" x 12" (229 x 305 mm) or 12" x 18" (305 x 457 mm) white or colored paper.

Fold the paper in half. Use the width of a ruler or one of the paper strips to draw a "stop" line across the open edge of the folded paper. Draw wavy lines from the line to the fold, then cut on the lines from the fold to the "stop" line.

Open the paper and weave strips through it. When weaving is finished, trace a heart on top of the woven product. Cut out the heart, **gluing as you go** (to avoid "broken hearts"). Glue pleated half- or quarter-doilies to back of the heart to make a lacy border, or pleat tissue or crepe paper around edge of the back.

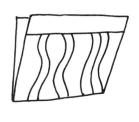
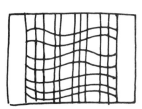
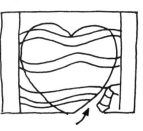

1 – red   5 – light purple
2 – yellow*   6 – pink
3 – light blue   7 – dark pink
4 – green

* The tiny centers of all the flowers are yellow.

TSD 2365-8 *The Elementary Calendar*

1 – red   5 – brown
2 – yellow   6 – black
3 – blue   7 – gray
4 – green   0 – white

TSD 2365-8 *The Elementary Calendar*

March Contents

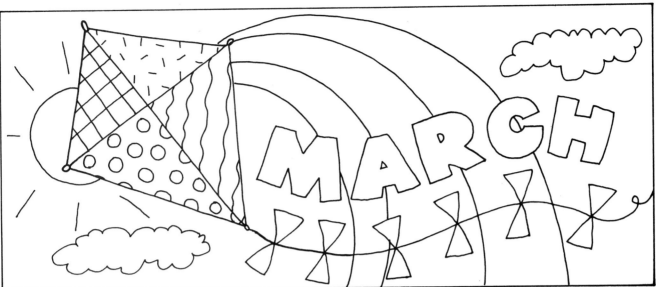

Sunday	Monday	Tuesday	Wednesday	Thursday	Friday	Saturday

MARCH BIRTHDAYS

2	Sam Houston	defeated Mexican forces at Battle of San Jacinto in order to win Texas from Mexico
3	Alexander Graham Bell	inventor of the telephone
6	Michaelangelo Buonarotti	Italian painter, sculptor, architect (1475–1564); *David*
7	Luther Burbank	horticulturist; developed new plant varieties
9	Yuri Gagarin	Russian cosmonaut; first man in space
	Amerigo Vespucci	America is named for this Italian explorer
10	Salvation Army	Christian organization established 1865
14	Albert Einstein	theoretical physicist; theory of relativity
15	Andrew Jackson	7th president
16	James Madison	4th president
18	Grover Cleveland	22nd and 24th president
19	David Livingstone	physician, missionary, explorer, "found" by Stanley
21	Johann Sebastian Bach	baroque composer; *Brandenburg Concertos*
24	Harry Houdini	world-famous magician and escape artist
25	Gutzon Borglum	sculptor of Mount Rushmore presidential portraits
26	Robert Frost	well-known American poet; "Stopping by Woods on a Snowy Evening"
	Sandra Day O'Connor	first woman nominated and appointed to the United States Supreme Court
29	John Tyler	10th president
30	Vincent van Gogh	famous Dutch postimpressionist painter; *Starry Night*
31	Franz Josef Haydn	Austrian classical composer; *London* symphonies
	Eiffel Tower	built for 1889 World's Fair in Paris

Poison Prevention Week

Look carefully at all the things in this room. Circle the things that are NOT poisons. Do you really KNOW which ones they are?

Only the bath soap, lipstick, shaving cream, and toothpaste are considered nontoxic by the American Family Health Institute. Everything else can cause poisoning.

POISON PREVENTION

The number of the nearest **POISON CONTROL CENTER** is:

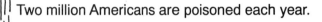

Two million Americans are poisoned each year.

- 90% of poisonings are accidental.
- 90% of poisonings happen at home.
- 70% of those poisoned are one- to five-year-olds.
- 80% of poisonings are by swallowing or eating.

That means:
MOST POISONINGS HAPPEN AT HOME WHEN CHILDREN SWALLOW SOMETHING THEY SHOULD NOT!

Inside the house . . .

Kitchen: dish detergents, cleaners, liquid spray cleaners, oven and drain cleaners

Bath: bathroom cleaners, prescription and nonprescription medicines—aspirin, cold medicines, etc.—first aid and health products

Bedroom: some cosmetics, nail and hair care products, often medicines

Laundry: detergents, bleaches, stain removers, starches and fabric softeners

Garage, Workshop or Basement:
gasoline, antifreeze, auto fluids, waxes, solvents, paints, glues, varnishes, turpentine, kerosene, weed and insect killers, fertilizers, pool chemicals

And outside . . .

leaves, berries, flowers, roots, stems, seeds, bulbs

What can you do to prevent an accidental poisoning?
- Watch little brothers and sisters carefully. They can get into even the most difficult-to-reach places and they will taste anything!

- If you think someone has swallowed something they should not have, find an adult fast! Ask them to call the Poison Control Center.

And remember the only rule you really need . . .
DO NOT PUT IT IN YOUR MOUTH!

MUSIC IN OUR SCHOOLS

Does your class sing in the morning?
Which song is it? Do you know all the words?

Can you hum a song from a movie? a play? a television show?

Play "Name That Tune." Whistle, hum, or play a few notes from any part of a familiar song. The person who guesses correctly hums or plays the next song.

Listen to different kinds of music. Radio stations offer many musical styles.

Write a song with a message: about safety, drugs, the environment, nutrition, etc.

Write a silly song: about an animal, an imaginary person, anything at all.

Draw a picture to go with a song.

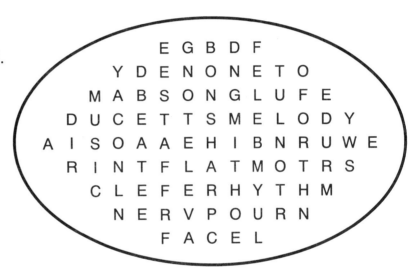

```
        E  G  B  D  F
     Y  D  E  N  O  N  E  T  O
     M  A  B  S  O  N  G  L  U  F  E
     D  U  C  E  T  T  S  M  E  L  O  D  Y
  A  I  S  O  A  A  E  H  I  B  N  R  U  W  E
  R  I  N  T  F  L  A  T  M  O  T  R  S
     C  L  E  F  E  R  H  Y  T  H  M
     N  E  R  V  P  O  U  R  N
        F  A  C  E  L
```

Does your school have a school song?

Find these music words:

MUSIC	CLEF	RHYTHM
MELODY	SONG	BEAT
NOTE	FLAT	STAFF
	HARP	

Write new words for a melody you already know.

Play "Repeat the Beat." Clap or tap a simple rhythm.
The next player must repeat your beat and add another, and so on.
(Clap-clap; clap-clap-clap; clap-pause-clap-clap)

And then there is always Musical Chairs!

March Is "Music in Our Schools" Month

March Is Youth Art Month

Duplicate the frame on this page and ask students to draw and color a picture—their favorite subject or one that you assign—inside. Let them color the frame, too.

SIMPLE FRAMES FOR STUDENT WORK

Choose colored paper slightly larger than the piece to be framed (or trim student's work).

Fold in quarters.

Cut outside edges in a simple design.

Cut folded corner to fit over work.

Tape or staple work to back of frame.

or

Fold paper in half and cut inside area in any simple, interesting shape.

Add yarn or glitter if you like.

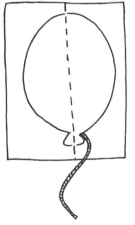
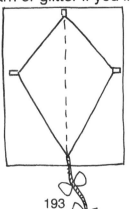

GOOD FOOD
FOR
GOOD HEALTH

NATIONAL NUTRITION MONTH

Dietary Guidelines for Americans

1. Eat a variety of foods.

2. Balance the food you eat with physical activity. Maintain or improve your **weight**.

3. Choose a diet with plenty of grain products, fruits, and vegetables.

4. Choose a diet low in fat, saturated fat, and cholesterol.

5. Choose a diet moderate in sugars.

6. Choose a diet moderate in salt and sodium.

Breads, Cereals, Rice, Pasta	6–11 servings a day
Vegetables	3–5 servings a day
Fruits	2–4 servings a day
Milk, Yogurt, Cheese	2–3 servings a day
Meat, Poultry, Fish, Dry Beans, Peas, Eggs or Nuts	2–3 servings a day

Condensed from *Dietary Guidelines for Americans*, 1995. U.S. Department of Agriculture, U.S. Department of Health and Human Services

WHAT'S NEW IN NUTRITION?

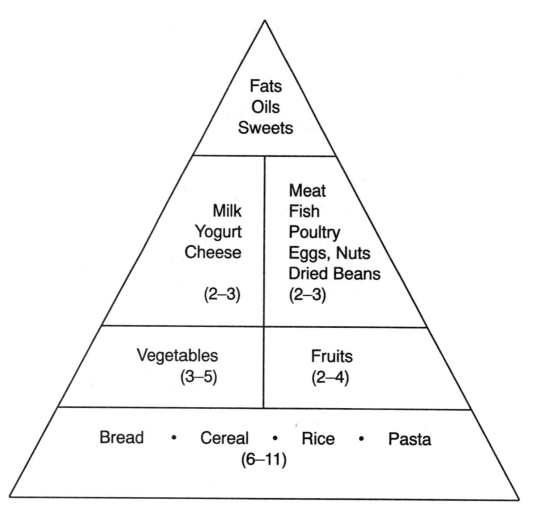

THE FOOD PYRAMID
(Recommended Daily Servings)

▲ The pyramid is a graphic representation of the revised Dietary Guidelines for Americans introduced in 1990.

▲ It shows a dramatic increase in the suggested intake of cereals and grain products which form the base of the pyramid.

▲ Recommended servings of vegetables and fruits have been increased slightly.

▲ While the dried beans/meat and the dairy groups appear near the narrowing top of the pyramid indicating a lower intake, the actual serving numbers remain the same.*

▲ Fats, oils, and sweets are a separate group to be "used sparingly," reflecting the continued concern over the amount of fat in the American diet.

* The pyramid made a brief public appearance in 1991, but was immediately withdrawn because of loud complaints from the meat industry.

WHAT'S NEW IN NUTRITION?

The Food Pyramid

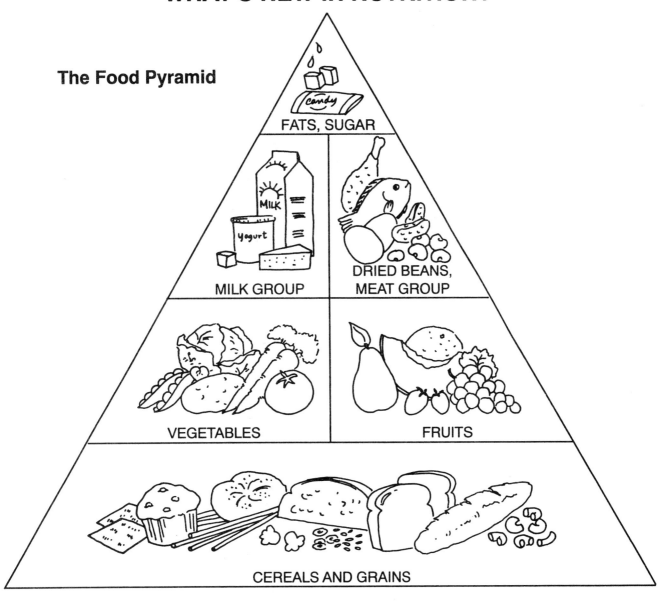

The Food Pyramid arranges the foods we eat in a triangle shape to show us how to eat a balanced diet.

▲ At the bottom, or base, of the pyramid are cereals and grains to show that we should "base" our diet on them. We should eat six to eleven servings a day—more than any other food group.

▲ The next two groups are vegetables and fruits, three servings (or more) of vegetables and two of fruits

▲ We should eat fewer servings from the milk and meat, fish, or dried beans groups—just two or three of each for adults. Children should have more milk.

▲ At the top of the pyramid is a tiny space for fats, oils, and sugar—things like butter, salad dressing, candy, and deserts.

▲ To be healthy, Americans need to eat more cereals, grains, and vegetables, but fewer meat and milk products. Americans should eat fewer fats and sugars.

The Food Pyramid

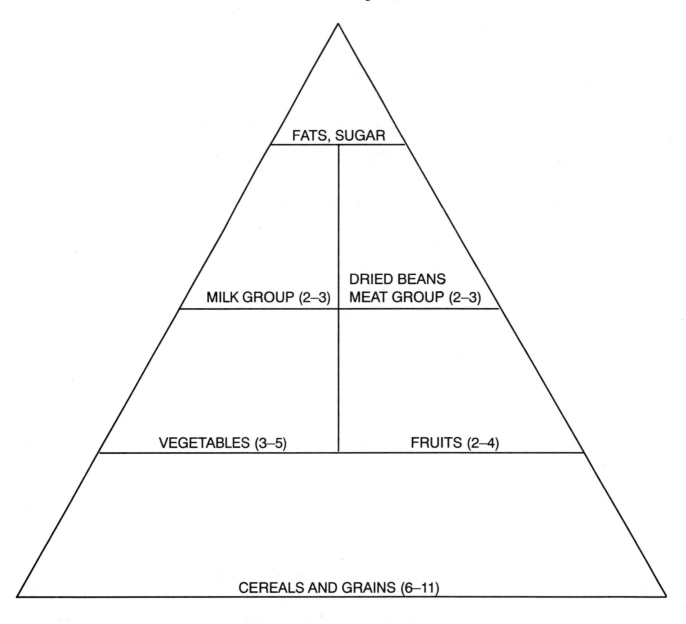

FATS, SUGAR

MILK GROUP (2–3)

DRIED BEANS
MEAT GROUP (2–3)

VEGETABLES (3–5)

FRUITS (2–4)

CEREALS AND GRAINS (6–11)

Cut out the food below and place them correctly on the pyramid.

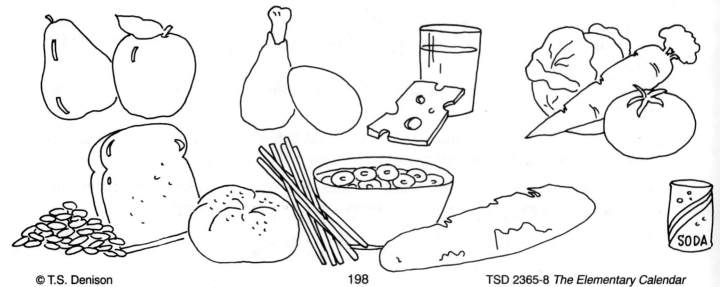

SODA

VEGETABLES AND FRUIT

Vegetables and Fruit

Put an X next to the vegetables and fruit you have tried. Put an XX if you liked it. Add to the list if you want.

_____	Asparagus	_____	Apples
_____	Green beans	_____	Bananas
_____	Lima beans	_____	Blackberries
_____	Beets	_____	Blueberries
_____	Broccoli	_____	Cantaloupe
_____	Brussels sprouts	_____	Cherries
_____	Cabbage	_____	Currants
_____	Cauliflower	_____	Cranberries
_____	Carrots	_____	Figs
_____	Celery	_____	Grapes
_____	Collards	_____	Grapefruit
_____	Corn	_____	Honeydew melon
_____	Cucumbers	_____	Lemons
_____	Eggplant	_____	Limes
_____	Kale	_____	Nectarines
_____	Lettuce	_____	Oranges
_____	Mushrooms	_____	Peaches
_____	Onions	_____	Pears
_____	Peas	_____	Plums
_____	Peppers	_____	Raspberries
_____	Potatoes	_____	Strawberries
_____	Pumpkin	_____	Tangerines
_____	Radishes	_____	Watermelon
_____	Rhubarb		
_____	Squash		
_____	Spinach		
_____	Sweet potatoes		
_____	Tomatoes		
_____	Turnips		
_____	Zucchini		

BREADS, CEREALS, GRAINS

TSD 2365-8 *The Elementary Calendar*

Name _____

Cereals and Grains

Put an X next to the cereal or grain products you have tried. Put an XX if you liked it. Add to the list if you want.

Breads

_____ Bagels
_____ Breadsticks
_____ Corn bread
_____ Date-nut
_____ French baguette
_____ Hamburger rolls
_____ Hard rolls
_____ Hot dog rolls
_____ Italian loaf
_____ Muffins
_____ Rye
_____ White
_____ Whole wheat

Rice

_____ Brown rice
_____ Rice cakes
_____ Fried rice
_____ Spanish rice
_____ White rice
_____ Wild rice

Pasta

_____ Lasagna
_____ Macaroni
_____ Noodles
_____ Pierogis
_____ Ravioli
_____ Spaghetti
_____ Ziti

Cereals

_____ Corn
_____ Cream of Wheat
_____ Grits
_____ Oatmeal
_____ Oats
_____ Rice
_____ Wheat

And

_____ Barley
_____ Fried noodles
_____ Kasha
_____ Matzoh
_____ Pie (crust)
_____ Pizza crust
_____ Taco shells
_____ Tortillas

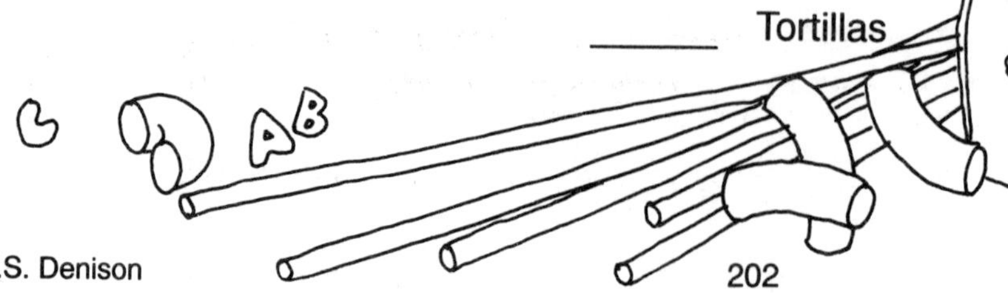

MILK AND DAIRY PRODUCTS

TSD 2365-8 *The Elementary Calendar*

Milk and Dairy Products

Pun an X next to the dairy products you have tried. Put an XX if you liked it. Add to the list if you want.

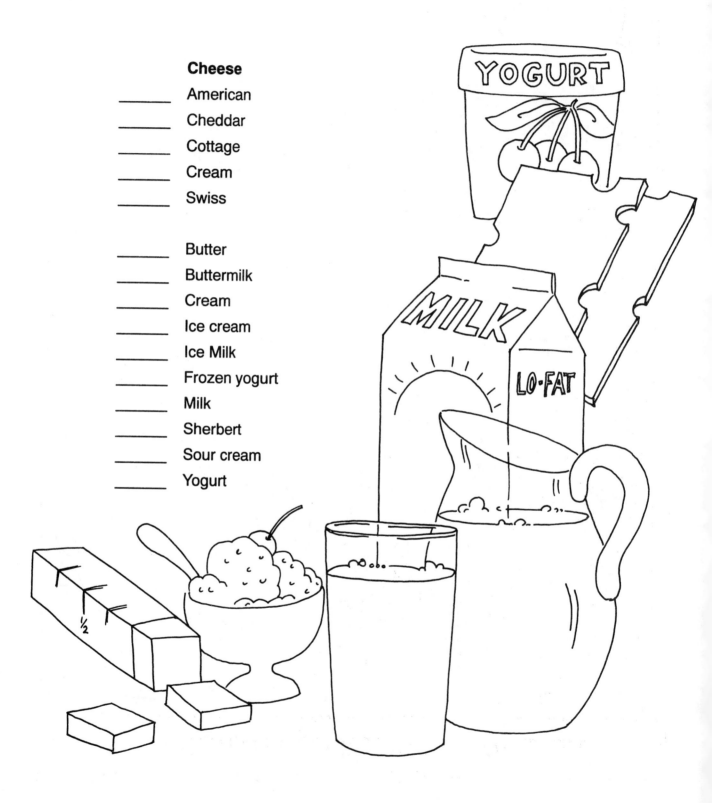

Cheese

_____ American

_____ Cheddar

_____ Cottage

_____ Cream

_____ Swiss

_____ Butter

_____ Buttermilk

_____ Cream

_____ Ice cream

_____ Ice Milk

_____ Frozen yogurt

_____ Milk

_____ Sherbert

_____ Sour cream

_____ Yogurt

MEAT, FISH, POULTRY, EGGS, NUTS, BEANS

TSD 2365-8 *The Elementary Calendar*

Meat, Poultry, Fish, Eggs, Dried Beans, Nuts

Put an X next to the meat group foods you have tried. Put an XX if you liked it. Add to the list if you want.

Meats

_____ Bacon
_____ Chicken
_____ Corned beef
_____ Duck
_____ Eggs
_____ Ham
_____ Hamburger
_____ Hot dog
_____ Goose
_____ Lamb chops
_____ Leg of Lamb
_____ Liver
_____ Meat loaf
_____ Pot roast
_____ Pork chops
_____ Pork roast
_____ Roast beef
_____ Sausage
_____ Spareribs
_____ Steak
_____ Turkey
_____ Veal

Dried Beans

_____ Kidney (chili)
_____ Baked beans
_____ Black Beans
_____ Black-eyed peas
_____ Lentils
_____ Navy beans
_____ Soy beans
_____ Split peas

Nuts

_____ Cashews
_____ Peanuts
_____ Pecans
_____ Walnuts

Seafood

_____ Fish (any kind)
_____ Clams
_____ Crabs
_____ Lobster
_____ Oysters
_____ Mussels
_____ Scallops
_____ Shrimp

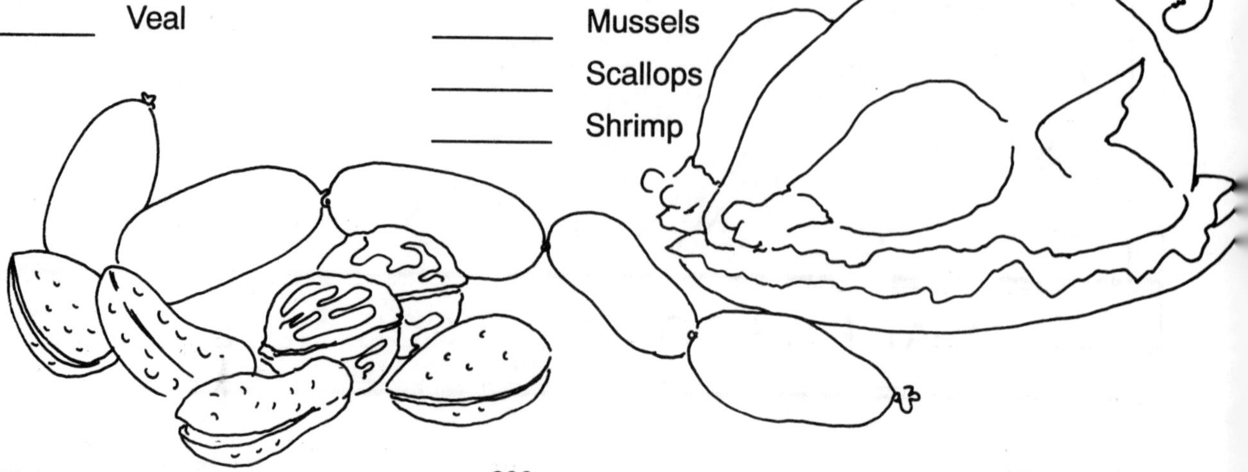

Name _____

Choose Foods from These Groups Every Day

Vegetables (3–5) Fruits (2–4)

Cereals and Grains (6–11)

Milk and Dairy Products

Meat, Fish, Poultry, Eggs, Nuts, Beans (2–3)

Breakfast	Lunch	Dinner

Teacher: Students may use this page to plan or record meals.

And Then There Are Snacks . . .

Watch out for these: salt, sugar, or fat.

Soda • Cake • Pie • Candy • Chocolate • Ice Cream • Cookies • Gum

CIRCLE THE SNACKS YOU EAT THE MOST

Fruit • Juice • Crackers • Raisins • Nuts • Popcorn • Cheese • Vegetables • Yogurt

Try more of these healthy snacks!

SNACKS CAN BE GOOD FOR YOU TOO!

Finish the face for each snack food.

Shopping for Snacks

Cut out the **healthy snacks** and fill the cart.

_____'s Supermarket

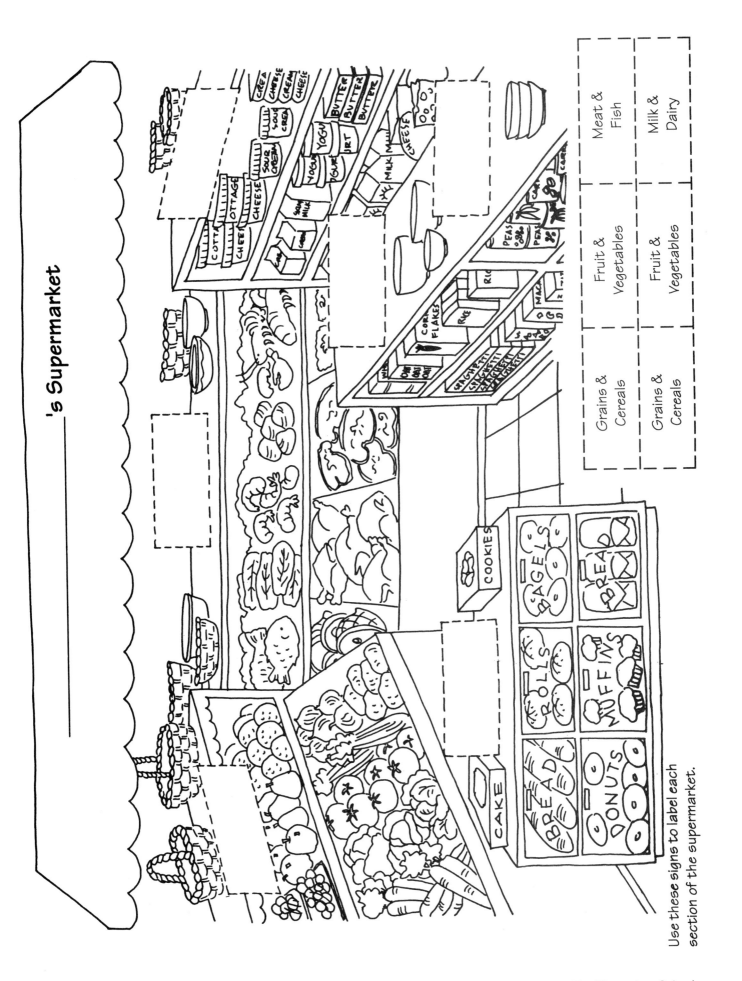

Meat & Fish	Fruit & Vegetables	Grains & Cereals
Milk & Dairy	Fruit & Vegetables	Grains & Cereals

Use these signs to label each section of the supermarket.

TSD 2365-8 *The Elementary Calendar*

At the Supermarket

Vegetables and Fruit

Cereals and Grains

Meat, Poultry, Fish, Eggs, Dried Beans

Milk and Dairy Products

Cut out the foods below and put them on the shelves where they belong.

The Four Food Groups

Circle the food that does not belong in the group. Color the pictures.

Fruits & Vegetables

Cereals & Grains

Milk & Dairy Products

Meat, Fish, Poultry, Dried Beans, Nuts, Eggs

Vegetables and Fruit

Put an X next to each fruit.
Draw a line from the food to its name.

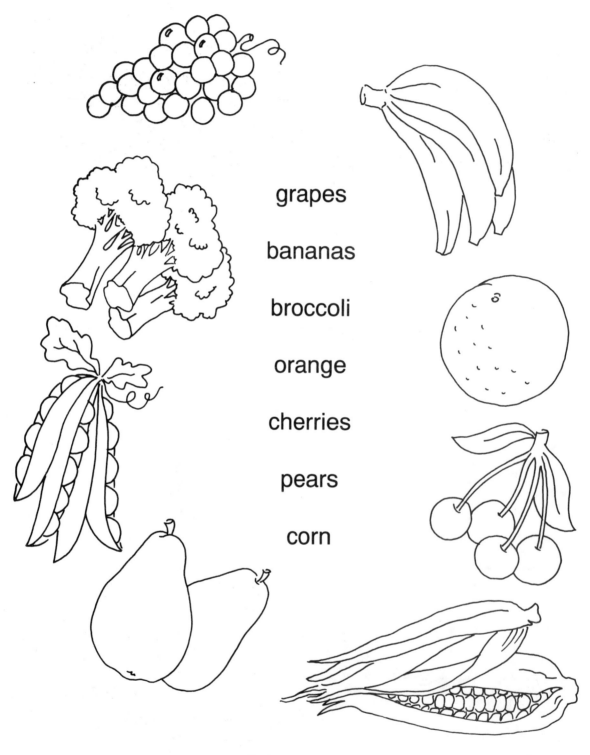

grapes

bananas

broccoli

orange

cherries

pears

corn

Color the pictures.

Putting it Together

Write G, V, D, or MB (Grain, Vegetable, Dairy, or Meat/Bean group) next to the ingredients.

PIZZA

_____ crust (dough)

_____ cheese

_____ tomato sauce

_____ sausage

_____ peppers, onions, mushrooms

TACO

_____ refried beans

_____ ground beef

_____ taco shell

_____ lettuce, tomato

_____ cheese

_____ sour cream

SANDWICH

_____ toast

_____ turkey

_____ Swiss cheese

_____ lettuce, tomato

_____ butter

PUTTING IT TOGETHER

Fill this sandwich with anything you like.
List your choices under the headings below.

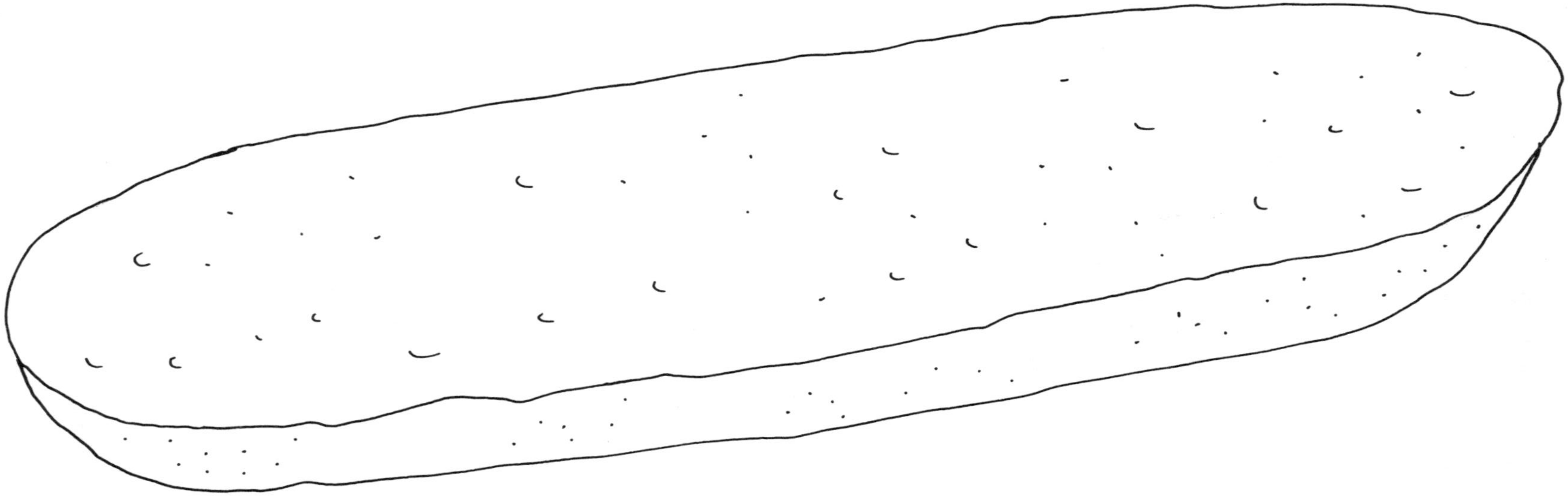

Grains	Vegetables	Eggs, Meat, Dried Beans	Dairy
6 foot loaf of bread!			

Name _____

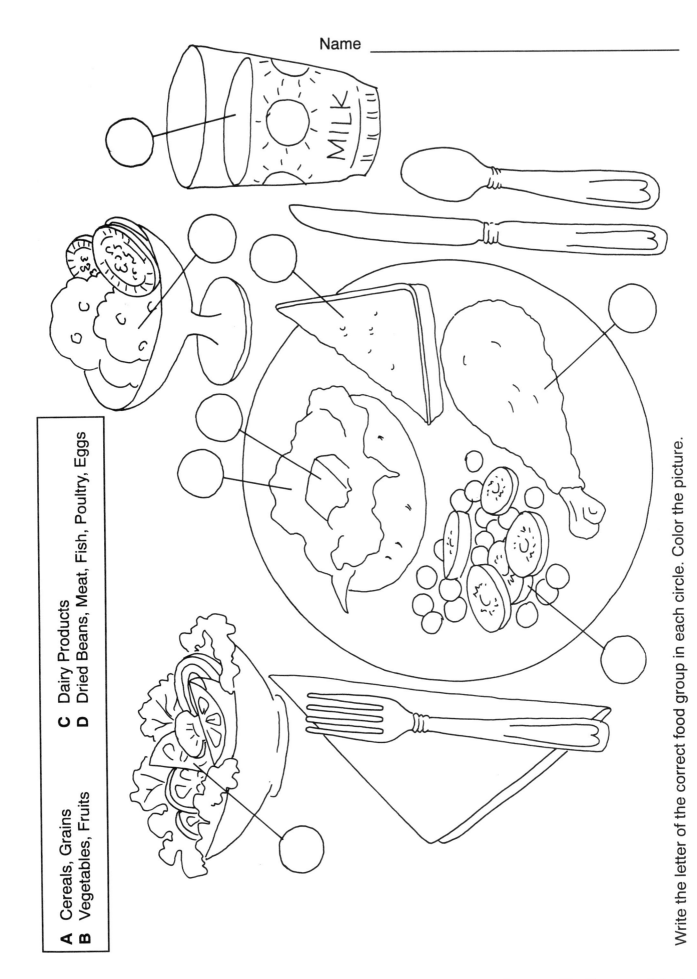

A Cereals, Grains
B Vegetables, Fruits

C Dairy Products
D Dried Beans, Meat, Fish, Poultry, Eggs

MILK

Write the letter of the correct food group in each circle. Color the picture.

TSD 2365-8 *The Elementary Calendar*

Good Eating Habits

Eat different kinds of foods.

Eat lots of vegetables, fruits, grains, and cereals.

Do not eat too much sugar, salt, or fat.

Stay at a healthy weight.

TSD 2365-8 *The Elementary Calendar*

Dinner Is Ready

1. red	6. dark green
2. yellow	7. light purple
3. blue	8. purple
4. dark blue	9. light brown
5. light green	10. dark brown

1. Butter and milk belong to the _____ group of foods.

2. The dinner roll is from the _____ group.

3. Grapes and lemons are _____.

4. Potatoes, onions, and broccoli are _____.

5. The hamburger belongs to the _____ group.

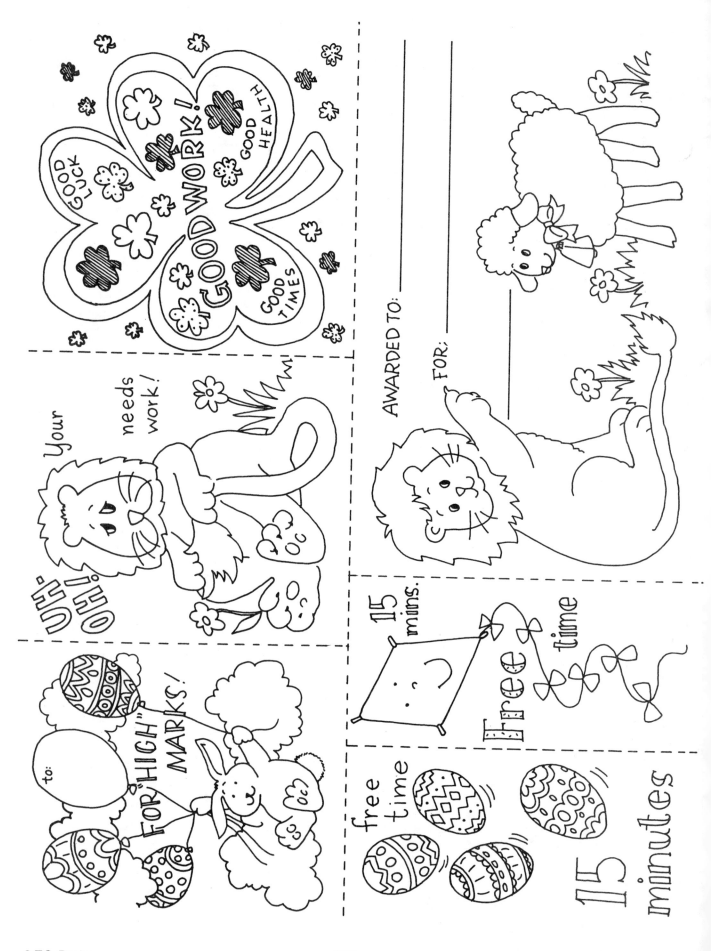

GOOD LUCK

GOOD WORK!

GOOD HEALTH

GOOD TIMES

Your needs work!

UH-OH!

FOR "HIGH" MARKS!

to:

AWARDED TO:

FOR:

15 mins.

Free time

free time

15 minutes

TSD 2365-8 *The Elementary Calendar*

```
        O B        O Z J
     A C F G I   I G L N I
     Z O W E A T H E R P Q S
     F T I U W X A B E D S E
     I F N B R E E Z E G H J
       K D L M O Q R N S A U
   A D F I V O W Y A B D F M
   I H L I O N W I B O O T S R I K J L
   L N A M P Q R B U N N Y W O Y C A B D
   O B M E G H I J E L M N O C O A T P O
   A B Q R S T P A T R I C K V N W Y Z
   S C D F P G H S I A J H L M D O P
   Q K T U V R W X T Y B Z I A C Y D I
   F E G G S I H J E K B L C M N O I
   Z T Q R T N U   R V I W K I T E X
     O Y Z A G       T B B F G I J
                     L M O P R I
                       J L M P
```

Find and circle these words:

SHAMROCK	GREEN	BUNNY	COAT
WIND	BLOW	EGGS	BREEZE
LION	SPRING	CANDY	WEATHER
LAMB	EASTER	BASKET	BOOTS
KITE	RABBIT	CHICK	ST. PATRICK

Use different colors to trace the strings. Then follow the directions at the end of the strings to color the kites.

Yellow, red,
orange, & green

Choose four
pretty colors

Orange, yellow,
blue, & green

Purple, green,
yellow, & orange

Red, white,
blue, & yellow

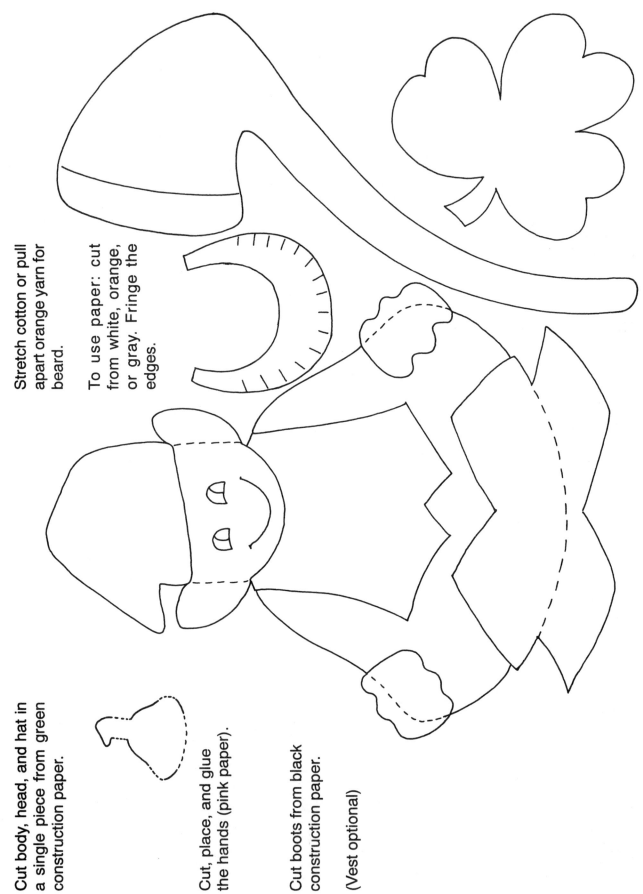

Stretch cotton or pull apart orange yarn for beard.

To use paper: cut from white, orange, or gray. Fringe the edges.

Cut body, head, and hat in a single piece from green construction paper.

Cut, place, and glue the hands (pink paper).

Cut boots from black construction paper.

(Vest optional)

Place the leprechaun on mushroom.

TSD 2365-8 *The Elementary Calendar*

Cut basic shape
of mane with
pinking shears

Cut the face and body from yellow construction paper and the mane from brown construction paper (or use other contrasting colors just for fun).

For tagboard pattern: Cut mane from body; trace on tagboard. Trim away mane and trace face. Trace body adding enough to pattern (dotted lines) to attach head.

Staple parts together for storage.

Leave tail attached on tagboard pattern to prevent tearing.

Cut body with large scallops.

Bell

Variation for face

For legs, use different color.

EASY LIONS AND LAMBS

Materials: sheets of 9" x 12" (229 x 305 mm) white, yellow, or brown paper; four pieces of 1" x 4½" (26 x 115 mm) black paper (for lamb); scissors; glue

Cut a wiggly oval as large as possible from a 9" x 12" (229 x 305 mm) piece of paper (white for the lamb, yellow or brown for the lion).

Use a 4½" (115 mm) heart-shape (right-side-up for lamb's face, upside down for lion's).

Round off corners of 1" x 2" (26 x 52 mm) piece for ears. Glue behind the head (leave the lamb's ears longer).

For lamb's legs, hold four 1" x 4½" (26 x 115 mm) black pieces together, and cut a triangle from one end for the hooves. Glue to back of lamb.

For faces, use any suitable color to contrast with body color.

Make a separate tail for lion or draw it on as shown.

PAPER BAG LION AND LAMB PUPPETS

Materials: paper lunch bags, colored construction paper

Precut construction paper rectangles for heads, bodies, and feet to fit the size of the paper bag. Use colors suitable to the animal.

Wiggle cut (or round off) rectangles as shown and glue on for head and body.

Provide heart pattern (or cut heart from folded paper) for faces.

Add ears (fold lamb's ears if desired) and feet.

Insert fingers in flap of bag to make puppet's head move.

- Be careful not to seal bag flap shut when gluing on head.
- Make "all-purpose eyes" and a simple triangle or heart noses from scraps.

EARLY BLOOMS

Materials: tissue, puffed rice cereal, popcorn, stamp pad, yarn, pencil, glue or paste, construction paper or wallpaper

Draw or use yarn to form branches in Y shapes.

Forsythia: Tear yellow tissue into small pieces, twist around end of pencil, dip in glue or paste and stick along branches.

Lilacs: Twist lavender or white tissue as for forsythia and bunch together in rough triangles.

Pussy Willow: Glue puffed rice cereal along stems or "finger print" them using stamp pad.

Variation: Use popcorn for snowball or wildflowers.

Fold construction paper or wallpaper in half and cut out vase if desired.

Make green leaves in appropriate shapes.

1 – red	5 – orange
2 – yellow	6 – purple
3 – blue	7 – pink
4 – green	8 – black

TSD 2365-8 *The Elementary Calendar*

April Contents

Sunday	Monday	Tuesday	Wednesday	Thursday	Friday	Saturday

TSD 2365-8 *The Elementary Calendar*

APRIL BIRTHDAYS

2	Hans Christian Andersen	Danish writer famous for fairy tales; "The Emperor's New Clothes"
3	Washington Irving	American author; "Rip Van Winkle," " Legend of Sleepy Hollow"
5	Booker T. Washington	African-American educator and leader; college founder
10	William Booth	founder of Salvation Army
13	Thomas Jefferson	3rd president
16	Charlie Chaplin Wilbur Wright	famous silent film comedian; *Modern Times* with brother Orville, aviation pioneer
18	Clarence S. Darrow	American criminal and political attorney; *Scopes Trial* (evolution)
21	Charlotte Brontë Friedrich Froebel	English novelist; *Jane Eyre* German educator; invented the kindergarten
23	James Buchanan William Shakespeare	15th president England's most famous playright and poet; *Romeo and Juliet*
26	John James Audubon	American artist and ornithologist
27	Ulysses S. Grant Samuel F. B. Morse Edward R. Murrow	18th president; commander of Union army contributed to invention of telegraph; created "Morse code" for telegraph famous and influential radio and television journalist
28	Lionel Barrymore James Monroe	famed actor of famous stage and film acting family 5th president

Mr. Dewey's Decimal System

Melvil Dewey invented a way to sort books so that we could find what we wanted to know quickly and easily in the library. He imagined a prehistoric person asking questions about the world and then he divided up the books to answer the questions.

100
Philosophy

Who am I?
Books about our minds and out thoughts.

200
Religion

How did the world and I get here?
Religious beliefs and myths

300
Social Sciences

Who is the person in the next cave?
Books about living together in groups, customs, careers, holidays, folklore, and fairy tales

400
Language

How can I make that person understand me?
Grammar and spelling books in many languages.

500
Pure Sciences

How do things work in the natural world?
Books about insects, animals, flowers, seashells, birds, rocks, and stars

600
Applied Sciences
(Technology)

How do other things work? Can I control nature?
Inventions, medicine, ships, cars, airplanes, pets, manufacturing, and food

700
Arts

How can I enjoy my time?
Books about painting, music, hobbies, theater, dance, humor, parties, and sports

800
Literature

What are the stories that people create?
Fiction, poetry, and plays

900
Geography and History

What have people done in the past?
Biography, geography, and history books

000
Generalities

Where can I get information in a hurry?
Encyclopedias, dictionaries, almanacs, and atlases

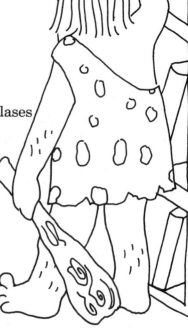

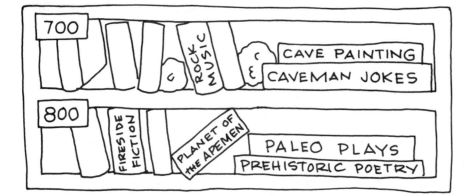

Name _____

National Library Week

Help the library staff get these new books ready for the shelves. Look at the titles and fill in the number that shows where the book belongs.

Five of the books show the authors' names. Put the first two letters of the author's name on the label too.

National Wildlife Week

WILDLIFE WORD SEARCH

Can you find these 24 animals hidden in the letters above?

DOLPHIN	GOOSE	BEAR	RABBIT
WHALE	DUCK	PUMA	SQUIRREL
SEAL	EAGLE	BUFFALO	CHIPMUNK
PENGUIN	FOX	DEER	OPOSSUM
FISH	LYNX	WOLF	SKUNK
SNAKE	RACCOON	COYOTE	BEAVER

Bonus: Find a house pet hiding with the wild animals. Circle it and write its name here: _____

Name _____

Keep America Beautiful Month

Litter makes our towns, cities, and highways look ugly, as if no one cared.

What's the best and safest thing to do? Clean up after yourself and after careless other people.

DO NOT LITTER!!!

A Litter Quiz for You

1. Do you put your own litter in the trash or in the proper recycling container? _____

2. Do you pick up litter in your classroom? _____ in the cafeteria? _____ in the hallways? _____ on the playground? _____

3. Do you pick up litter even if you did not put it there? _____

4. Do you take a litter bag on car trips, when camping, or to the beach? _____ and use it? _____

5. Do you pick up litter when you see it in your neighborhood? _____

Ask your teacher about taking a "Litter Walk" to clean up the playground or a park near your school.

If you try to do these things, you are a "Litter-ary Success!"

Give yourself this award.

ALEXANDER'S SING-ALONG LITTER SONG

(To sing while you are cleaning.)

Pick it Up!

If you see a piece of litter,
Pick it up! Pick it up!
If you see a piece of litter,
Pick it up!

Because litter makes a mess,
And you can't do any less.
If you see a piece of litter,
Pick it up!

If it's on the grass or sidewalk,
Pick it up! Pick it up!
If it's on the grass or sidewalk,
Pick it up!

What's the difference if you did it?
Put it in the trash and lid it.
If you see a piece of litter,
Pick it up!

Oh, I wish there were no litter,
Anywhere! Anywhere!
Oh, I wish there were no litter,
Anywhere!

Come on every boy and girl,
We can make a better world!
Don't you wish there were no litter,
Anywhere?!

Now you make up a verse,
(It sure cannot be any worse)
As you sing and work along . . .
Pick it up!

To the tune of "If You're Happy (and You Know It)"

Keep America Beautiful

Help clean up this park! Put a piece of white paper over the picture. Take the picture to a window and trace it on the white paper. Do not trace the weeds and litter! Leave them out of your beautiful park!

To the teacher: Students may draw in their own shrubs, flowers, and trees; add swing sets, birds, animals, etc., to the finished picture. Use the other side of this page to create a "surprise" picture.

Keep America Beautiful

Put your Clean Park picture over this page and trace again at the window.
Look at the difference we can make!

TSD 2365-8 *The Elementary Calendar*

HERE'S GOOD NEWS!

Recycling of glass, aluminum, tin, and newspaper is becoming more evident every day.

Recycling of plastics has begun with manufacturers coding containers for sorting purposes.

One-third of our paper mills use waste paper exclusively.

Recycled paper products are widely available if you look for them.

Paper towels and toilet paper are often made from recycled paper.

Over 75% of recycled boxes are made into new ones.

A recycled aluminum can is processed and back in the stores within six weeks.

About 50% of the raw material used in steel production comes from scrap.

People are becoming more aware; in 1988, San Diego county expected 16,000 Christmas trees for recycling—they received 97,000.

Japan recycles half its household and commercial waste. The United States only recycles 10%, but is improving.

Making Every Day "Earth Day"

Three easy-to-read and -understand paperback books for you, your classroom, and the school library:

50 Simple things You Can Do to Save the Earth
50 Simple Things Kids Can Do to Save the Earth
The Recycler's Handbook

50 Simple Things Kids Can Do to Save the Earth has a great many activities. The other two books have a devastating ecological fact at the bottom of each page. All three are informative and fascinating, and all three were compiled by The EarthWorks Group, in Berkeley, California.

In addition to information from your local agencies and organizations, try these:

- *To stop future junk mail, keep your name from being sold.*
  Write to:
  Direct Marketing Assoc.   or   Mail Preference Service
  6 E. 43rd Street   Direct Marketing Assoc.
  New York, NY 10017   11 W. 42nd Street, P.O. Box 3861
                                                              New York, NY 10163-3861

- *Free information on paper reuse and recycling:*
  American Recycling
  American Paper Institute
  260 Madison Avenue
  New York, NY 10016

- *To replace all those trees, help plant 100 million by 1992:*
  American Forestry Association
  Global Releaf Program
  P.O. Box 2000
  Washington, DC 20013   (202) 667-3300

- *For a list of products that use recycled packaging and a booklet, send $2.00 to:*
  Pennsylvania Resource Council
  25 W. 3rd Street
  Media, PA 19063

- *To help save the rainforest:*
  The Rainforest Action Network
  301 Broadway, Suite A
  San Francisco, CA 94133   (415) 433-1000

- *For a book list and information on backyard wildlife:*
  National Wildlife Federation
  Backyard Wildlife Habitat Program
  1412 16th Street NW
  Washington, DC 20036-2266

- *On recycling aluminum, fund-raising, statistics, etc.:*
  Aluminum Association
  900 19th Street NW
  Washington, DC 20006   (206) 862-5100

- *Free pamphlets on glass recycling:*
  Glass Packaging Institute
  1801 K Street NW
  Washington, DC 20006   (202) 887-4850

- *Catalog of recycled paper products and free handouts:*
  (10% of company profits goes to environmental organizations)
  Earth Care Paper Co.
  P.O. Box 3335
  Madison, WI 53704

- *Ecology and Balloons*   (send SASE):
  Balloons and Clowns
  703 N. Milwaukee Avenue
  Libertyville, IL 60048

- *For information on beach cleanup projects:*
  Center for Marine Conservation   and   The Oceanic Society
  1725 DeSales Street NW   218 D Street, SE
  Washington, DC 20036   (202)429-5609   Washington, DC 20003

- *To help "stamp out styrofoam"*   (send SASE):
  The Ecology Center
  2530 San Pablo Avenue
  Berkeley, CA 94702

  "McFact" Pack   ($5.00):
  Citizens Clearinghouse for Hazardous Waste
  P.O. Box 926
  Arlington, VA 22216   (703) 276-7070

- *Free Newsletter, "Pet Projects"*
  (This is about plastics made from petrochemicals, not about puppies and kittens.):
  NAPCOR (National Association for Plastic Container Recovery)
  4828 Parkway Plaza Blvd., Suite 260
  Charlotte, NC 28217   (800) 7-NAPCOR

- *For Teachers*
  Free recycling study guide: *How-to guides for classroom recycling:*
  Recycling Education Coordinator   The Information Center (05-305) US EPA
  Bureau of Information and Education   401 M Street SW
  Department of Natural Resources, P.O. Box 7921   Washington, DC 20360
  Madison, WI 53707

Books for Kids and Their Parents

*Child's Play: 200 Instant Crafts and
Activities for Preschoolers*
Leslie Hamilton
NY: Crown Publishers1989

*50 Simple Things Kids Can Do to
Save the Earth*
The Earth Works Group
Berekley, CA: Earthworks Press 1990

*Garbage! Where it Comes From,
Where it Goes*
Evan and Janet Haddingham
NY: Simon and Schuster Books for Young
Readers in Association with WGBH Boston,
1990

A Kid's Guide to How to Save the Planet
Billy Goodman
NY: Avon Books, 1990

*Let's Grow: 72 Gardening Adventures
with Children*
Linda Tilgner
Storey Communications, 1988

*Recyclopedia: Games, Science, Equipment,
and Crafts from Recycled Materials*
Robin Simons
Boston: Houghton Mifflin, 1976

*Treat the Earth Gently: An Environmental
Resource Guide*
Sherrill B. Flora
Minneapolis: T.S. Denison, 1991

Name _____

Signs of the Times

Look for these signs on bottles and bags and boxes. You will find them on many packages made from paper or plastic.

The recycle sign inside a circle means that this box, bag, or bottle was made from used paper or plastic. You will find this sign on boxes of cereal, crackers, cookies, and anything else that comes in a box.

I found this sign on _____ .

This recycle sign means the package was made from new paper or plastic, but it could be used again for a new package if we recycle it. You will find this sign on plastic bottles and paper bags.

I found this sign on _____ .

This sign is only used on plastic containers. The number tells what kind of plastic was used to make the package so that a recycling center could send it to the right place to be used again.

I found this sign on _____ .

Ten Easy Things Kids Can Do To Save the Earth
(and ten more for Mom and Dad)

Even Very Little Kids Can . . .

1. Pick up litter (even if they did not put it there).
2. Work carefully and use both sides of the paper whenever they can.
3. Pick up six-pack rings and snip them (or rip them).
4. Help recycle at home.
5. Eat cereal that comes in recycled boxes.
6. Hold on to balloons (or have moms or dads tie the balloons to their wrists).
7. Learn how to save water and energy at home.
8. Help feed the birds in winter.
9. Reach for a rag instead of a paper towel.
10. Refuse a bag for a small item.

And They Can Ask Mom and Dad to . . .

1. Take their own bags to the grocery store.
2. Buy juice in cans or bottles, not boxes ("brick-packs" cannot be recycled).
3. Look for the "recycled material" symbol when they shop.
4. Try to buy and use less plastic (and reuse it when they do buy it).
5. Use containers for storage instead of paper, foil, and plastic wrap.
6. Try not to buy or use things made from Styrofoam.
7. Remember to recycle at home and at work.
8. Use the microwave or toaster oven to save energy.
9. Use water-based paint, markers, and glue.
10. Read books and watch programs about how to take care of the earth.

There! That makes twenty. What a good way to begin. Find out more that you can do!

Name _____

Reuse – Recycle – Reduce

Contains Recycled Paper

Can Be Recycled

Look for this symbol on packages of cereal, cookies, crackers—anything that comes in a box. It means the box was made from re-cycled paper. Sometimes the symbol is black in a white or colored circle. Recycled boxes are gray inside.

Look for this symbol on paper bags, boxes, and containers not made from paper, such as plastics. It means the container *could* be recycled. It does not mean that the company used recycled material to make the package or container, or even that there is a place that can recycle it.

Look around you! Make a list of some of the things you find in your kitchen. Write the names in the columns below. Which products do you think your family should buy more often?

Packages With the Recycled Symbol	Packages With No Symbol or "Please Recycle" (*Hint:* Look in the freezer too.)

Name _____

SAVE THAT TREE

Look at the picture. Circle the things that are made from paper. Are any of these things recycled in your community? Put an R next to the things that are recycled.

Now use these words to fill in the sentences below.

PAPER NAPKIN   PAPER TOWELS   PAPER CUP   PAPER PLATE

PAPER BAGS   TISSUES   NEWSPAPERS

1. Instead of _____, I could use a handkerchief to blow my nose.

2. I could use a plate and wash it afterward instead of using a _____ .

3. I could use a cloth napkin instead of a _____ .

4. An old rag is good for cleaning up spills and saves _____ .

5. Many towns recycle _____ after we finish reading them.

6. I could use a favorite mug or glass instead of a _____ .

7. _____ can be used again when Mom and Dad shop for groceries.

The Problem Is Not Plastics, It Is People

Here are some good things about plastic:
1. It is light in weight so it costs less to ship from factory to store.
2. It keeps foods and medicines clean and safe.
3. Lightweight plastic car parts help us to use less gas and oil.
4. It protects us from accidents because it does not break easily.

And here are the bad things
1. Many plastics are not "biodegradable." That means they do not break down and cannot go back into the earth. They stay around forever.
2. We use too much of it even when we do not need it.
3. We throw too much of it away without even thinking about it. We buy "disposable" things and then we just throw them out.

Look around you! Look at home, at school, in the store.
Now try this activity.

Plastic "Disposables" I Found	Something We Could Use Instead

Remember: A few plastics are recyclable and biodegradable.
Some plastics are not biodegradable, but they are recyclable.
Some plastics are neither recyclable nor biodegradable.

Name _____

We Have Your Number!

Some communities have recycling programs for all plastic containers. Others ask people to sort plastic things by the numbers on the bottoms of the containers.

Look around you! See if you can find containers like these. Look for the number on the bottle, tub, lid, or liner. Write the number in the circle of the container in the picture that matches it.

TSD 2365-8 *The Elementary Calendar*

For the Teacher

You may get different answers for the numbers below, but in general, laundry and cleaning products = 2; squeeze bottles = 4 or 3; clear deli tubs = 5, but the lid may be a 4; Styrofoam egg cartons = 6; soda bottles = 1, although the number may not be evident—look for a tiny, round blister.

Older children may write the names of the products on the pictured containers as well as filling in the numbers.

The point? Awareness. Very little recycling is being done with the higher numbers. A number 7 is not recyclable at all.

Let's Sort it Out

Alexander is recycling, every thing that he can get.

Help Alexander recycle. Draw lines to put these things in the right containers. The soda bottle, too, please—when it is empty!

PAPER, PLASTIC, AND PACKAGING
TOO MUCH OF A GOOD THING

Packaging helps us. It keeps food and medicine and other things clean and safe . . . BUT . . .

Some things have too much packaging—too many paper and plastic wrappers.

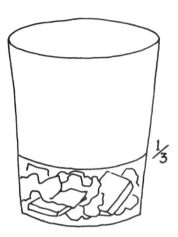

PACKAGING IN OUR TRASH

PACKAGING WE THROW OUT RIGHT AWAY

Circle the packages that have too many wrappers.
Draw a line from those packages to the same things, but with less wrapping.

TSD 2365-8 *The Elementary Calendar*

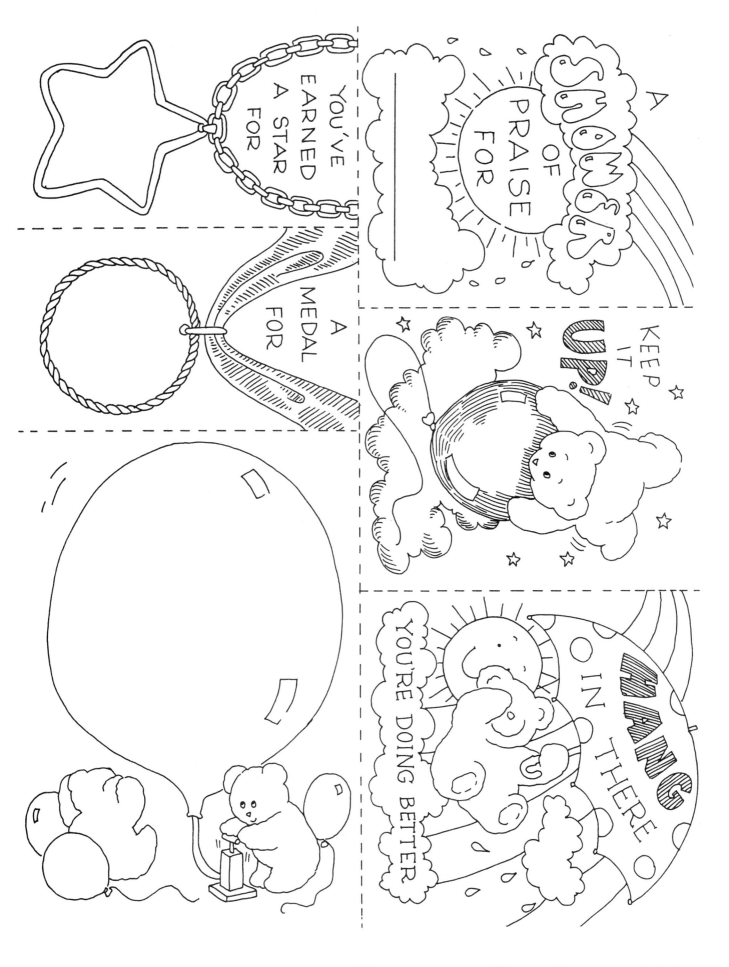

YOU'VE EARNED A STAR FOR

A SHOWER OF PRAISE FOR

A MEDAL FOR

KEEP IT UP!

HANG IN THERE

YOU'RE DOING BETTER

TSD 2365-8 *The Elementary Calendar*

Name _____

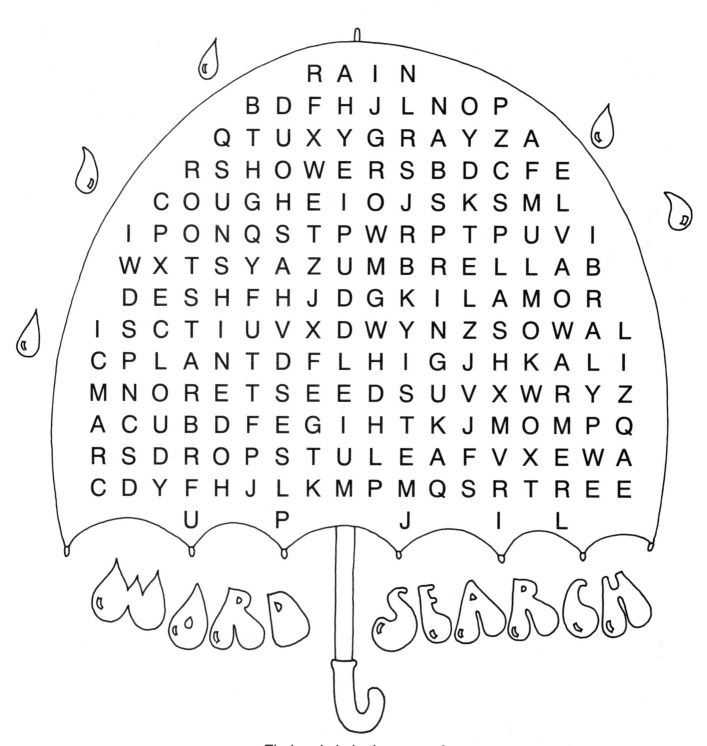

```
            R A I N
        B D F H J L N O P
      Q T U X Y G R A Y Z A
    R S H O W E R S B D C F E
    C O U G H E I O J S K S M L
  I P O N Q S T P W R P T P U V I
  W X T S Y A Z U M B R E L L A B
  D E S H F H J D G K I L A M O R
I S C T I U V X D W Y N Z S O W A L
C P L A N T D F L H I G J H K A L I
M N O R E T S E E D S U V X W R Y Z
A C U B D F E G I H T K J M O M P Q
R S D R O P S T U L E A F V X E W A
C D Y F H J L K M P M Q S R T R E E
    U     P         J     I   L
```

Find and circle these words.

SHOWERS	CLOUDY	LEAF	WET
RAIN	PLANT	TREE	SOW
SPRING	SEEDS	ROOTS	GRAY
WARMER	DROPS	PUDDLE	SUNSHINE
STEM	GROW	SPLASH	UMBRELLA

Name _____

TSD 2365-8 *The Elementary Calendar*

Name _____

EASTER EGGS

Materials: Styrofoam or blown eggs, wallpaper or construction paper, glue

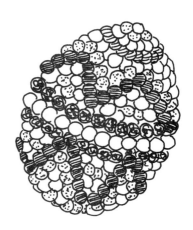

This idea takes time, but is easy and very effective. Let children use any free time to work on their eggs.

Punch dots from wallpaper or construction paper and glue on an egg in overlapping patterns. Young children can make multicolored polka-dot eggs without specific patterns.

Use round styrofoam balls to adapt this idea for Christmas.

STAND-UP TUBE BUNNY

Materials: cotton or cotton balls, construction paper

Precut construction paper in your choice of colors. We suggest white or brown with pink.

    6" x 9" (152 x 229 mm) – body
    3" x 4½"(76 x 115 mm) – paws (4)
    6" (152 mm) square – head
    2" x 4½" (52 x 115 mm) inside ears (2)

Round off corners of 6" x 9" (305 x 457 mm) paper, then center vertically on 12" by 18" (152 x 229 mm) sheet.

Fold 6" (152 mm) square paper in half, then round off all but one fold corner. Open and glue in place for head.

Shape outer and inner ears by rounding corners of proper rectangles (above). Glue to back of head.

Round off the corners of all four paw rectangles at once. Place and glue as shown leaving arms free except at shoulders. Use scraps for features and whiskers. Round onto tube, staple, and add a cotton tail. Bend up feet to stand.

QUILLING

Materials: toothpicks, jar lids, paper, glue

Cut paper into strips 3 (76 mm) and 4 (102 mm) inches wide. Then cut into very thin (¹⁄₁₆" or 2 mm) strips, 3" (76 mm)- and 4" (102 mm-long. Roll strips carefully and smoothly around cylindrical toothpicks pinching gently where necessary to form the shapes shown.

A shallow jar lid lined with paper makes a nice frame.

For shapes formed from a circle, roll around toothpick, remove and release slightly. Glue outside end to keep shape and pinch to make designs (without flattening inner circles).

Use toothpick to apply glue to edges and form into various designs.

Young children may use wider strips and a pencil.

BASKETS

Materials: Assorted sizes and colors of paper (square and rectangular shapes), scissors, glue or staples

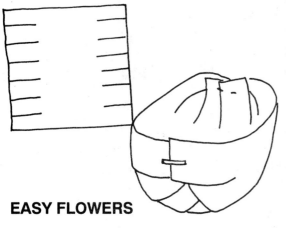

Fringe opposite edges of paper in wide strips as shown. Gather strips together (beginning in the middle and working outward) and glue or staple as shown. Alternating strips from each side of the center gives a neater look but is not necessary. Add a paper strip handle and use for flowers, eggs, etc.

EASY FLOWERS

Materials: colored paper, scissors, glue

Fold any size paper square into quarters.

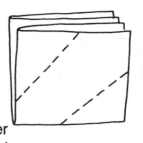

Cut petal shapes as shown, being careful not to cut the corner that will become the flower center (the one between the fold and the double fold). Use singly or stack in progressively smaller sizes and glue in interesting combinations of shape and color. Make centers from punched paper dots or crumpled tissue.

To make stems: use same method as for Egg Carton Tulips below or simply add green strips and leaf shapes if flowers are to be mounted flat.

EGG CARTON TULIPS

Materials: Plastic egg cartons in various colors, pipe cleaners, plasticine, spray can tops, tissue scraps, scissors, glue

Cut plastic egg cups apart, then cut or fringe edges into floral petal shapes. Fold tissue scraps several times, fringe ends and wrap pipe cleaner tightly around center. Poke pipe cleaner through top of cup and pull through until fringe is in flower center.

Add a leaf by folding ends around stem and gluing to itself. (Pipe cleaners resist white glue.)

For flower pots, collect spray can tops. Push small lump of non-hardening clay (or plasticine) into bottom of cap and stick in flower. Make a bouquet!

TSD 2365-8 *The Elementary Calendar*

1 – red   6 – purple
2 – yellow   7 – light brown
3 – light blue   8 – light purple
4 – orange   9 – white
5 – green

May Contents

Sunday	Monday	Tuesday	Wednesday	Thursday	Friday	Saturday

MAY BIRTHDAYS

4	Horace Mann	educator; "Father of education in the United States"
6	Robert E. Peary	Arctic explorer
8	Harry S. Truman	33rd president
9	John Brown	abolitionist; led attack on Harpers Ferry
11	Salvador Dalí	leading surrealist painter; *Soft Watches*
12	Florence Nightingale	English founder of modern nursing procedures
15	Lyman Frank Baum	American newspaperman and author; *The Wonderful Wizard of Oz*
16	William Henry Seward	negotiated purchase of "Seward's Folly" (Alaska)
18	Dame Margot Fonteyn	famed British ballerina
20	Dolley Madison	celebrated first lady; wife of President James Madison
24	Brooklyn Bridge	opened 1883 after fourteen years of building
25	Ralph Waldo Emerson	American essayist and poet; *Nature*
26	Sally Ride	first American woman astronaut; third woman in space
	Isadora Duncan	pioneer dancer who revolutionized concept of dance
27	Rachel Carson	scientist; book *Silent Spring* led to DDT ban
29	John F. Kennedy	35th and youngest president; assassinated November 22, 1963
	Patrick Henry	American revolutionary author/orator: "Give me liberty, or give me death."
31	Walt Whitman	beloved American poet; *Leaves of Grass*

This is a nice space for students to write (neatly!) a brief essay on Why I Appreciate My Teacher. Offer them the option of writing about last year's teacher.

National Pet Week

DO YOU HAVE A PET?

My pet is a _____. Its name is _____.

I take care of my pet by _____.

If you have other pets, tell what they are and their names: _____

_____

Be Kind to Animals Week

Take good _____ of your pet.

Feed the _____ in winter.

Words you will Materials: hurt, birds, care, litter

Do not _____.
Animals can get hurt.

Do not tease or _____ animals.

Alexander's Operation

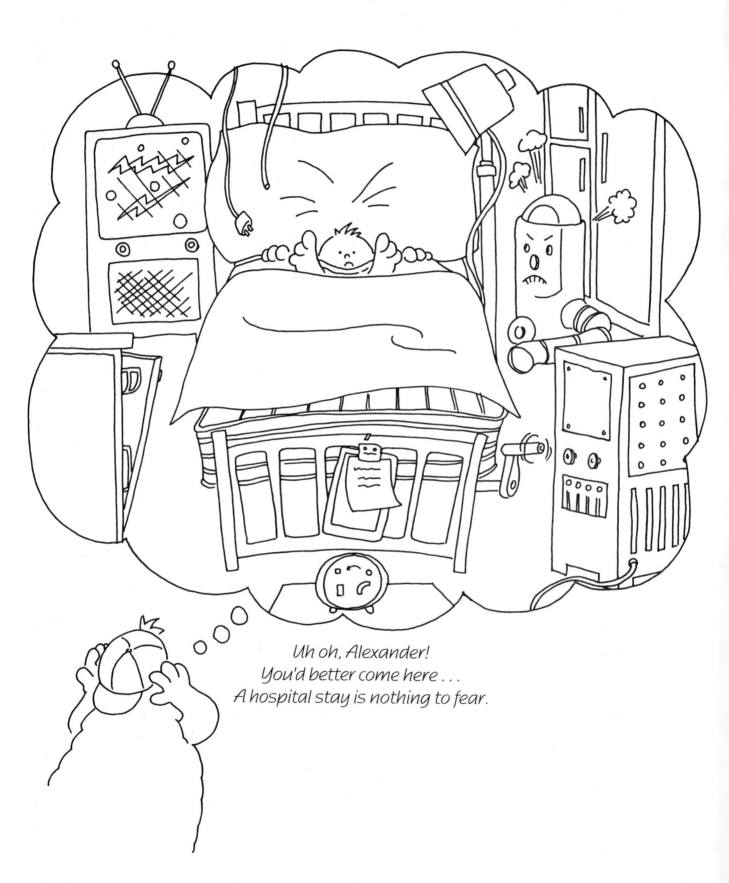

Uh oh, Alexander!
You'd better come here . . .
A hospital stay is nothing to fear.

We will get some good books,
That were written to tell,
Just how a hospital,
Helps kids to get well!

Our hospital has
A good program, too,
Showing kids and their parents,
What hospitals can do.

And then we'll go home
To pack what you'll need;
Some pj's, a toothbrush—
A good book to read?

And here you are
All settled down,
Name bracelet to wear,
And a hospital gown.

TSD 2365-8 *The Elementary Calendar*

So many people!
And strange things to do!
But you know all about it.
It's not really new.

And here's the big morning.
I'm right by your side.
As off to the o.r.
You go for a ride.

You're being so good!
(I knew you could do it.)
Don't worry my dear,
You'll sleep right through it!

And now here your are.
Back in your room.
What's that you said?
"Over so soon?"

TSD 2365-8 *The Elementary Calendar*

Yes, it's all over,
and now you'll be well.

Very soon you'll be home
with a story to tell!

Good books: *Going to the Hospital* by Fred Rogers
    Why Am I Going to the Hospital by Claire Ciliotta and Carol Livingston

MOTHER'S DAY BOUQUET

Materials:
Styrofoam egg cartons (in different colors)
plastic or metal caps (from detergent, cleaning sprays, etc.)
scraps of yellow tissue paper
scraps of green tissue or construction paper
pipe cleaners (greens and yellows are best)
modeling clay
scissors
white glue

 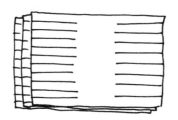 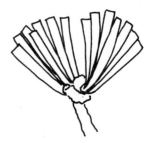

1. Cut egg carton apart and fringe cups any way you like.

2. Hold together two or three pieces of yellow tissue and fringe the ends.

3. Twist the end of a pipe cleaner tightly around the center of the fringed paper.

4. Push the other end of the pipe cleaner through the bottom of an egg cup flower.

5. Press a lump of modeling clay into the bottom of the "flower pot."

6. Cut long leaves from green tissue or construction paper and glue around stems.

 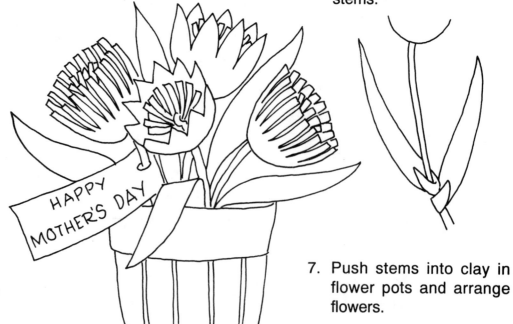

Add a tag if you like, or make a card.

7. Push stems into clay in flower pots and arrange flowers.

Mother's Day Card

Copy, color, fold, and write message inside.
Variation 1: Cut away dark areas after folding.
Variation 2: Copy two to a page, cut apart, trim away darker areas and glue to a 9" x 12" (229 x 305 mm) piece of construction paper in a spring color.

POLICE OFFICERS AROUND THE WORLD

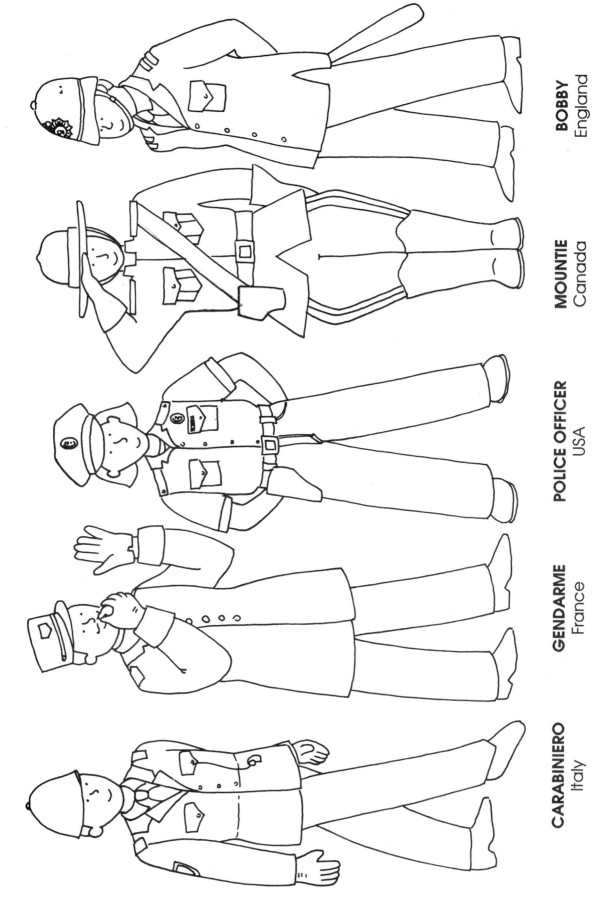

BOBBY
England

MOUNTIE
Canada

POLICE OFFICER
USA

GENDARME
France

CARABINIERO
Italy

Police officers all over the world work to help people and to protect the laws of their countries.

Are You a Couch Potato?

COUCH POTATO

No muscles or bones in Couch Potato.
He's let them waste away.
He'd rather snack and watch TV
Than run and jump and play.

If you want to be a Couch Potato,
There's really nothing to it.
But if it's fitness that you're after,
GET UP, GET OUT and DO IT!!

Sports Spuds

No couch potatoes here!
These spuds are enjoying sports!
How many sports can you find in the picture? What are they?

Name _____

Find the things in this picture that can be noisy.
Mark them with an X. *Hint:* There are twelve noisy things.
Color the picture. Think of other things around that can be noisy.

TSD 2365-8 *The Elementary Calendar*

Name _____

"Use It, or Lose It"—Safely

Our bodies need exercise, but safety is important, too. Broken bones, sprains, and strains are often caused by carelessness about safety. When doing physical work or exercising, use your head as well as the rest of your body!

◆ Falls can break your bones and damage muscles. Obey teachers, coaches, and other adults in charge of activities. Obey safety rules when:
   • Riding your bike
   • Playing sports
   • In the gym
   • On the playground
◆ Do only what you can.
   • Do not try to lift things that are too heavy for you.
   • Do not try to run farther or faster than you easily can.
   • Give yourself exercise warm-up and cool-down periods.
   • "No pain, no gain" is not true. If it hurts, do not do it.

Write a safety rule for:

1. Preventing a fall from your bike.

2. A playground activity you enjoy.

3. Playing a sport you like or about which you know.

I Know About My Bike . . .

Write the number of each part in the correct circle on the diagram below.

1. seat
2. frame
3. handlebar
4. reflectors
5. chain
6. pedal
7. chain guard
8. tire

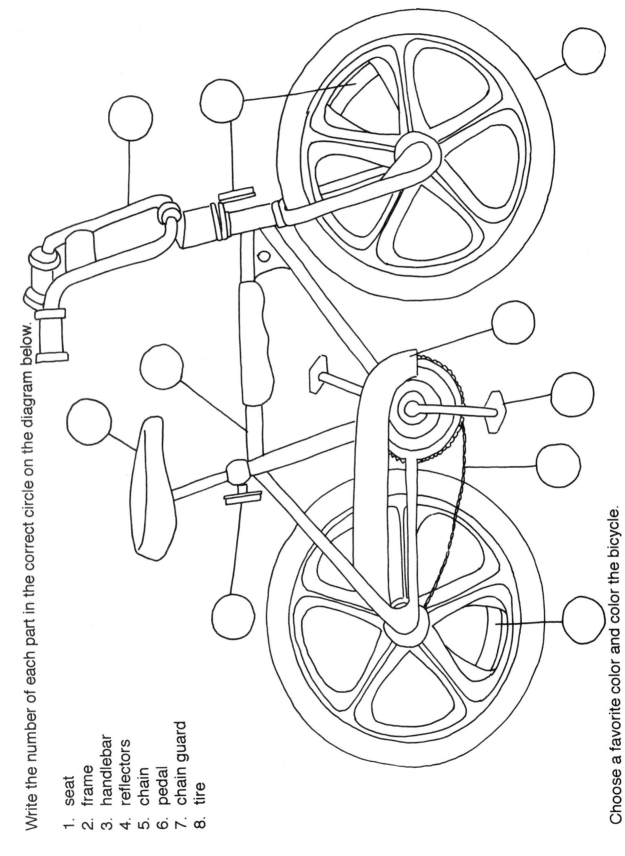

Choose a favorite color and color the bicycle.

Name _____

Use Your Head! . . . Put a Helmet On It!

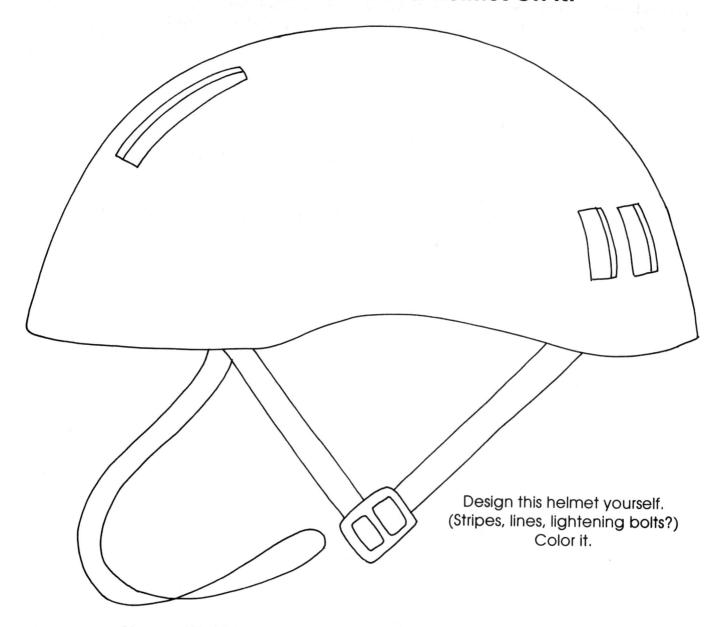

Design this helmet yourself.
(Stripes, lines, lightening bolts?)
Color it.

Here are the four things that cause the most bicycle accidents.
Have you ever done any of them? Answer YES or NO.

Have you ever . . .

1. _____ entered the road without stopping and looking for cars?

2. _____ entered an intersection without obeying traffic signs or signals?

3. _____ swerved left in front of a car suddenly and without warning?

4. _____ ridden against traffic or without hands?

Senior Citizens (Older Americans) Month

This is the month to show our appreciation for the older Americans we know—grandparents, neighbors, and family friends. Here are a few ways you can show you care, not just throughout this month, but all year long.

If you live near an older American:
- Offer to help with the yard and garden, especially weeding. Older people sometimes have trouble getting up and down.
- Offer to shovel the walk in winter and to salt or sand it for their safety.
- Respect their property. Stay out of the yard unless you are invited. Many senior citizens try to keep their yards looking nice.
- Play quietly (or somewhere else) if you know they nap in the afternoon.
- Offer to pick up a few items at the local convenience store if you are allowed to go there.

If you are visiting a senior citizen:
- Hands off! Older people may have had a lamp, a vase, or a knickknack for many years. You would feel awful if you broke it and so would they.
- Be polite. Say "please" and "thank-you."
- Offer to find, fetch, or carry things. Your legs are younger.

If you know someone in a hospital or nursing home, or even if you do not, your class or scout troop can:
- Arrange for short visits to sing, play games, or put on a program. (Think of the elderly throughout the year, not just at Christmastime.)
- Make holiday decorations or arrange to display school art projects to brighten the halls and dining room of a nursing home.
- Collect and cut out pictures (from magazines, calendars, cards). Glue them to construction paper and make booklets of flowers, animals, pretty scenes, or cartoons. Even someone with poor eyesight can enjoy looking at bright, happy pictures.

And in General:

- Be courteous and patient.

- Some senior citizens love children and will want to fuss over you—be patient. Some feel uncomfortable with children—respect their feelings.

- Speak up, speak clearly, and look at an older person when speaking. Some older people do not hear very well.

- Be ready to repeat what you have said. Some older people forget easily. Do not say, "But I just told you!" Just say it again—politely.

- Move carefully. Many senior citizens have trouble walking and are afraid of falling. Scampering around like a squirrel upsets and frightens them.

Show you care. Older Americans, or senior citizens, have lived a long time and have seen and experienced many things. They deserve our care, our courtesy, and our respect every day of the year.

YOU CAME THROUGH

A GREAT PERFORMANCE

GREAT

in _____

by _____

You did well today!

TSD 2365-8 *The Elementary Calendar*

Name _____

A C B D G F I
C L O W N G A H J K
L I M P N W A R M O C P
S Q R T U F V W D Z Y O X I
J E K C L M L N O E P B U D Q
R E S U T S O I L N U V N W Y
X D Z S A C W B D F E G T H J I
K S L N O M E G H P J L R K M N
O P M E M O R I A L D A Y Q F R
S L O V E W Y X Z A I B D C L I
E F T G H J I R I N G K C L A
I B H O E C E A G T F H A J G
O E K L N M K O P R Q R S
R T V U L E A V E S D I
I W Z X B D C A E

Find and circle these words:

FLOWER	CIRCUS	HOE	CARD
GARDEN	CLOWN	RAKE	COUNTRY
WARM	RING	SOIL	LOVE
SEEDS	BUD	LEAVES	FLAG
PLANT	DIG	MOTHER	MEMORIAL DAY

All but one of the flowers have a matching partner.

Name _____

Pattern

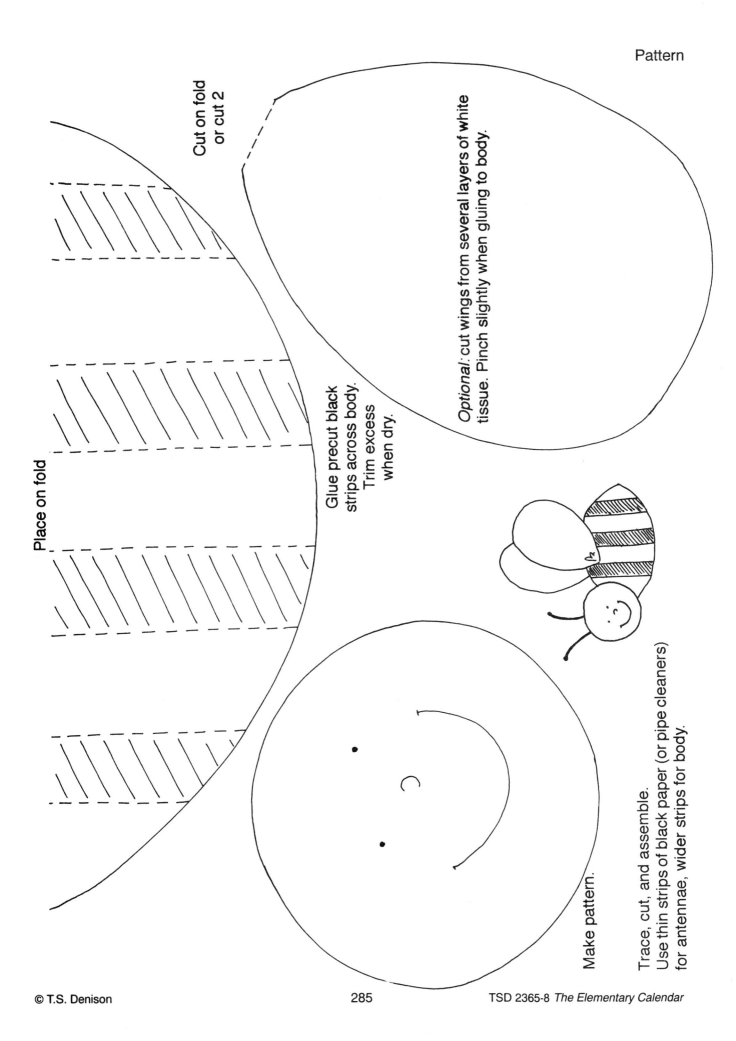

Cut on fold
or cut 2

Place on fold

Optional: cut wings from several layers of white tissue. Pinch slightly when gluing to body.

Glue precut black strips across body. Trim excess when dry.

Make pattern.

Trace, cut, and assemble. Use thin strips of black paper (or pipe cleaners) for antennae, wider strips for body.

Butterfly

For full butterfly,
place on fold (12" x 18 or 305 x 457 mm)

Place on fold

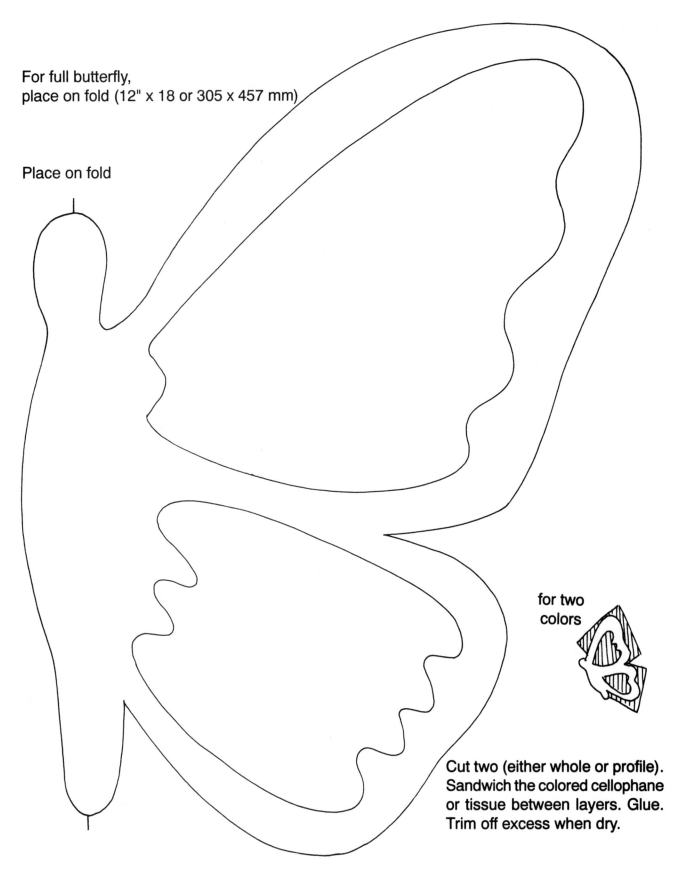

for two
colors

Cut two (either whole or profile).
Sandwich the colored cellophane
or tissue between layers. Glue.
Trim off excess when dry.

SEED MOSAICS

Materials: dried seeds and beans, 6" (152 mm) square newsboard (cardboard), 6" (152 mm) square colored construction paper, pencil, glue

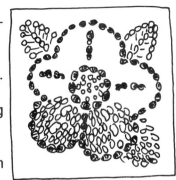

Lightly draw a simple design on the construction paper. Glue to newsboard.

Outline and fill design with beans and seeds in a variety of colors using white glue.

* Use only one kind of bean or seed for outlining each shape so the design will not be lost.

PAPER SCULPTURE FLOWERS

Materials: petal pattern, colored construction paper, scissors, pencil, glue

Trace and cut out a few petal patterns.

Open scissors and use one blade to "draw" (score) a line down the middle of the petal. Fold away from scored side. Glue only tips of petals around flower center.

To make centers and bell flowers: Cut small circles (the inside handle of the scissors is good for this) and clip to center. Form into shallow cup as shown and glue point or side to paper.

Use petal pattern for leaves.

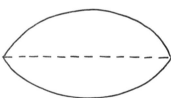

JUNGLE FLOWERS

Materials: green and white craft paper, watercolors, brushes, scissors

Using crayons, start flower "growing" from center dot on 12" (305 mm) square white paper. Make a ring of simple designs around center. Letters of the alphabet repeated and/or alternated work well for design elements.

Build another ring out of the first and continue making concentric rings to edge of paper. Paint lightly with watercolor and wiggle-cut around edge when dry. If you prefer not to paint, use many colors in crayon or marker.

Draw long curving stem and leaves with black crayon on green craft paper (about 36" x 10" or 914 x 254 mm). Add veins and "bugs."

Cut out stem and leaves in one piece and glue or tape to the back of the flower.

1 – red
2 – yellow
3 – light blue
4 – orange
5 – green
6 – purple

Color the flower petals as you like or leave them white.

June Contents

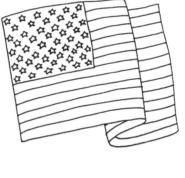

YOUR ENVIRONMENT

YOUR RESPONSIBILITY

Sunday	Monday	Tuesday	Wednesday	Thursday	Friday	Saturday

JUNE BIRTHDAYS

3	Jefferson Davis	only president of the Confederate States of America
8	Frank Lloyd Wright	famous American architect; organic architecture (natural materials); *Fallingwater, The Guggenheim Museum*
9	Cole Porter	prolific/popular lyricist and composer
	Donald Duck	1934
12	George Bush	41st president
14	Harriet Beecher Stowe	writer; her *Uncle Tom's Cabin* "began" Civil War
	United States Army	1775; first United States military service
26	Pearl S. Buck	known for novels set in China; Nobel Prize for Literature; *The Good Earth*
27	Helen Keller	author, lecturer; blind, deaf advocate for help for the handicapped
	Happy Birthday song	1924; Mildred and Patty Hill

Name _____

OUR PLEDGE TO THE FLAG

I pledge allegiance to the flag
of the United States of America
and to the Republic for which it stands,
one Nation under God, indivisible,
with liberty and justice for all.

FLAG FACTS
Rules and Customs of Our Flag

Did you know that . . .?

★ The American flag should fly outdoors only from sunrise to sunset or be spotlighted.
★ The American flag is raised quickly and lowered slowly—to show that we are eager to see it fly and sorry to take it down.
★ The American flag should not touch the ground, floor, or brush against other objects.
★ The American flag should never be used for decorating or covering anything. It must always fly freely. The design may not be used on anything that we buy or use in our homes.
★ The American flag is never flown below another flag except for the flag of the United Nations and the church pennant raised when the navy holds religious services at sea.

QUESTIONS FOR FLAG DAY

1. How many stars does our flag have today? _____

2. Which two states added the last two stars to our flag?

   _____ and _____

3. How many rows of stars are on our flag today? _____

4. Does each row have the same number of stars in it? _____

5. What color is the top stripe of the flag? _____

6. How many red strips are there? _____ How many white? _____

Flag Day – June 14

1776

The first American flag that looked a little like our flag of today was called the "Continental Colors" It had thirteen stripes, one for each of the colonies. In the upper left hand corner was the British Union Jack, the crosses of Saint George and Saint Andrew. The stripes showed our pride in America and the British Union showed our loyalty to England.

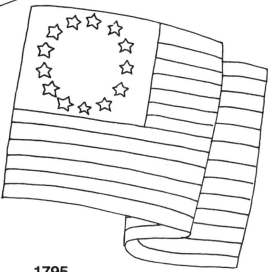

1777

Then came the Revolutionary War and America needed a flag of its own. The Continental Congress decided on thirteen stripes of red and white and a blue field with thirteen white stars. Congress did not say how the stars should be arranged so there were many designs. The one we know best is called the *Betsy Ross Flag* because many people believe that she made it.

1795

In 1791 Vermont joined the union; Kentucky followed in 1792. To show these two new states, the flag called "Old Glory" was designed with fifteen stripes and fifteen stars. This was the flag that Francis Scott Key wrote about in the "Star Spangled Banner."

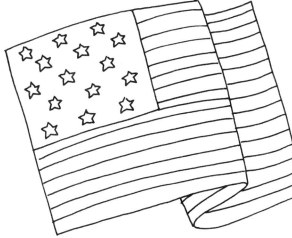

1818

As new states wanted to join the union, Congress realized that adding a new stripe for every state would spoil the design of the flag and make it much too big. They decided to return to thirteen stripes (seven red and six white) to represent the original colonies, and to add a star for each new state.

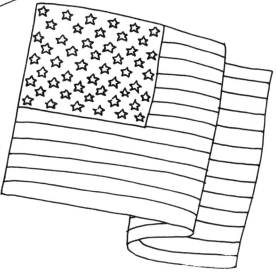

This is still the design of our flag.

Father's Day Shirt

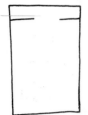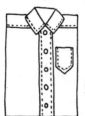

Materials: 9" x 12" (229 x 305 mm) colored and white construction paper; scissors; colored markers, crayons or colored pencils; glue

Precut construction paper of various colors in half, lengthwise, for ties; make tagboard patterns for tie.

Fold white paper about 1¾" (45 mm) down from the top to get a straight line. Open and cut fold on each side about one-third toward center.

Fold top corners down and glue in center to form collar as shown. With one color of a marker, crayon, or colored pencil, draw two lines from the collar to the bottom of the paper. Add two lines for yoke. Using the same color, "stitch" the shirt as shown adding a pocket and buttons.

Design the pattern by repeating and alternating colors to make plaids or stripes. The older the child, the more complex the pattern may be.

Choose a color from the pre-cut papers. Trace the tie on one side of the paper. Save scraps for a handkerchief.

Decorate the tie and glue under shirt collar. Cut a sample handkerchief and write a Father's Day message on it. Carefully poke a hole with scissors and cut open top of pocket. Insert the handkerchief.

For very young children: Precut collars on white paper (cut several at once) and omit handkerchief.

Variation: **Jacket with Shirt and Tie**

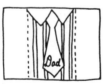

Fold 9" x 12" (229 x 305) paper in thirds as shown, overlapping slightly.

Fold back top corners and cut out a square from each to form lapels. Add pockets, buttons, stitching and fabric pattern as desired.

Open paper and draw a large W for collar; design shirt pattern. Add tie cut from colored construction paper (or tie may be drawn).

Write message on either side of shirt.

Try making the shirt at the top of this page using 6" x 9" (152 x 229 mm) white construction paper. Make the jacket in brown, gray, blue, etc., and insert shirt, having collar and tie show through lapels.

Father's Day Card Activity

"Leave" These Alone!

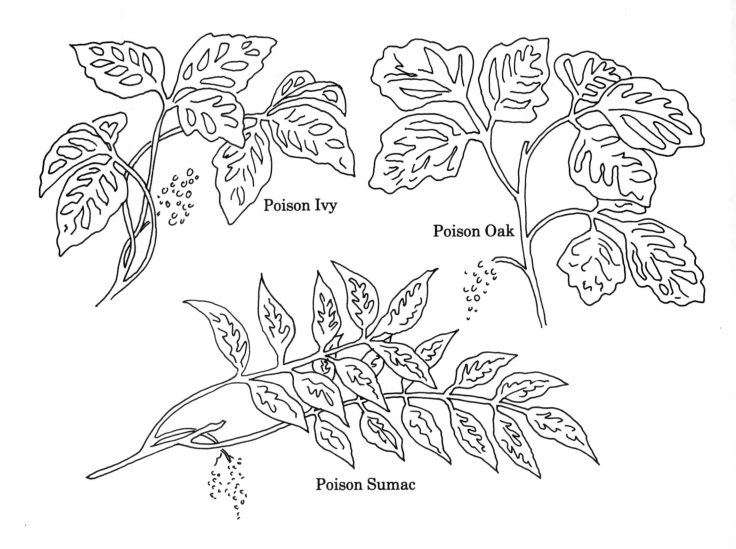

Poison Ivy

Poison Oak

Poison Sumac

Poison Ivy has three leaflets per leaf. They may be smooth and shiny, but not always. The leaves are green. Usually dark and glossy; the berries are grayish-white. Poison ivy grows anywhere!

Poison Oak is very much like poison ivy, but its leaves are a little rounder. It grows on the west coast and the southeastern United States.

Poison Sumac is more toxic than the other two plants and very tempting in the fall because of its beautiful orange and red leaves. Poison sumac has grayish-white berries; harmless sumacs have red ones. Poison sumac grows in wet places.

If you think you have touched a poisonous plant, quickly wash the area with strong soap and lots of water. The oil of the plant causes the itching and blistering and it must be removed. After you wash thoroughly, using rubbing alcohol. If you still get an itchy rash or blisters, calomine lotion will help the itch. For a bad case, you must see a doctor.

Alexander's Rules for Water Safety

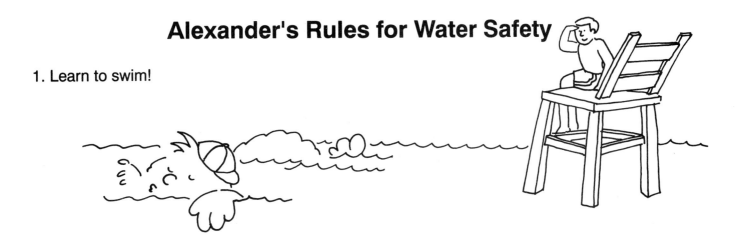

1. Learn to swim!

2. Swim only in guarded or supervised areas.

3. Never swim alone! Use the buddy system for safety.

4. Do not dive except where it is permitted and supervised.

5. Obey pool and beach safety rules.

6. Wear a life jacket when boating or fishing

7. Stay seated in a boat. If you must move, stay low and move carefully.

8. Get permission from your parents before enjoying water sports.

9. Let your parents know where you will be (and with whom) and be there!

10. Enjoy your summer—safely!

TSD 2365-8 *The Elementary Calendar*

YOUR ENVIRONMENT

YOUR HOME

YOUR NEIGHBORHOOD

YOUR TOWN AND STATE

YOUR COUNTRY

YOUR WORLD

YOUR RESPONSIBILITY

TSD 2365-8 *The Elementary Calendar*

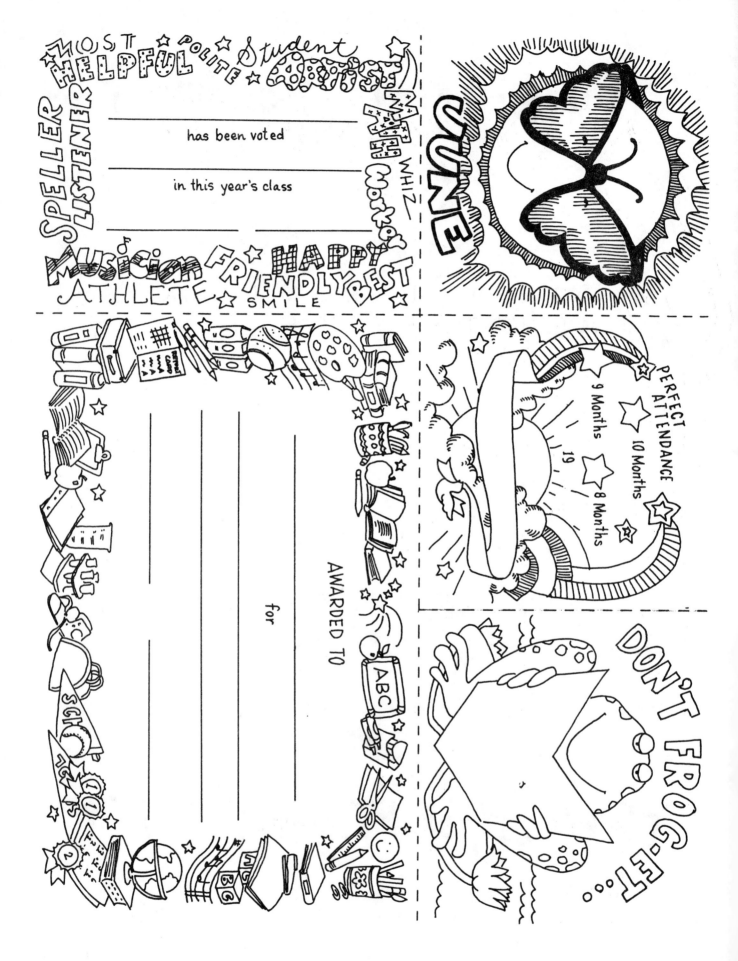

MOST HELPFUL POLITE Student ARTIST
SPELLER LISTENER MATH WHIZ Worker
MUSICIAN FRIENDLY HAPPY BEST
ATHLETE SMILE

_____

has been voted

_____

in this year's class

_____   _____

JUNE

PERFECT ATTENDANCE
9 Months
10 Months
19
8 Months

DON'T FROG-ET...

AWARDED TO

for

_____

NAME _____

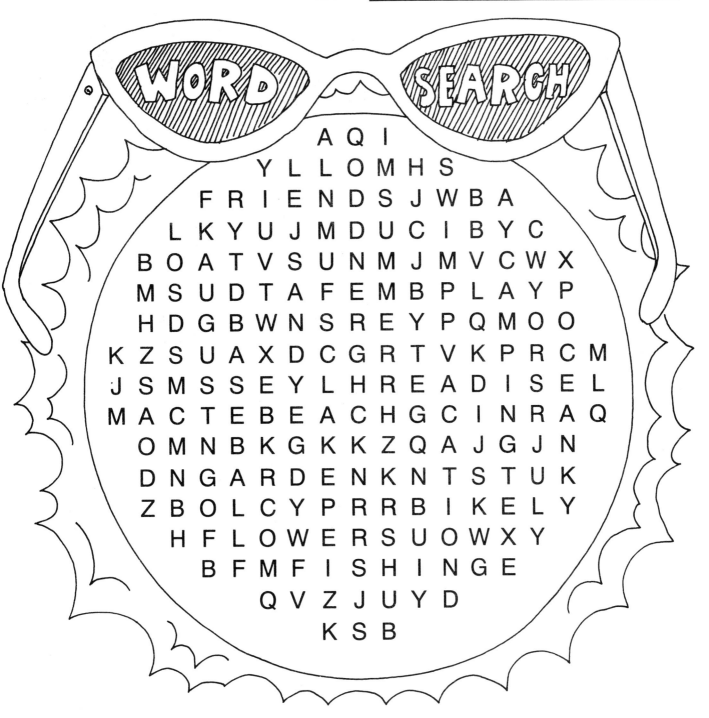

```
          A Q I
        Y L L O M H S
     F R I E N D S J W B A
   L K Y U J M D U C I B Y C
 B O A T V S U N M J M V C W X
 M S U D T A F E M B P L A Y P
 H D G B W N S R E Y P Q M O O
K Z S U A X D C G R T V K P R C M
J S M S S E Y L H R E A D I S E L
M A C T E B E A C H G C I N R A Q
 O M N B K G K K Z Q A J G J N
 D N G A R D E N K N T S T U K
 Z B O L C Y P R R B I K E L Y
   H F L O W E R S U O W X Y
     B F M F I S H I N G E
       Q V Z J U Y D
          K S B
```

Find and circle these words in the letters above:

SUMMER	FRIENDS	GARDEN	VACATION
PLAY	SWIM	LAKE	BASEBALL
READ	CAMPING	SUN	SAND
AUGUST	BOAT	FLOWERS	BIKE
FISHING	JULY	BEACH	OCEAN

   TSD 2365-8 *The Elementary Calendar*

Name _____

10 Things I Enjoyed About This Year!

PLAYS — CONCERTS — GYM — SCIENCE — LANGUAGE

TRIPS — PARTIES — ART — MUSIC — HOMEWORK — COMPUTERS

MY CLASS — GAMES — HISTORY — LEARNING — SINGING — TEACHERS — LUNCH — MATH — MUSEUMS — BOOKS — LIBRARY — HEALTH — READING — IDEAS — NEWS

Here is a mini-picture of something I enjoyed this year.

This Summer Maybe I Will

1. _____

2. _____

3. Read _____

4. Go _____ with _____

5. Help Mom by _____

6. _____ 7. Eat _____

8. Write _____

9. See _____

_____

_____

10. Wear _____

11. Help my _____ by _____

12. Play _____ with _____

13. Help Dad _____

14. _____

15. Enjoy _____

Name: _____

BALLOON

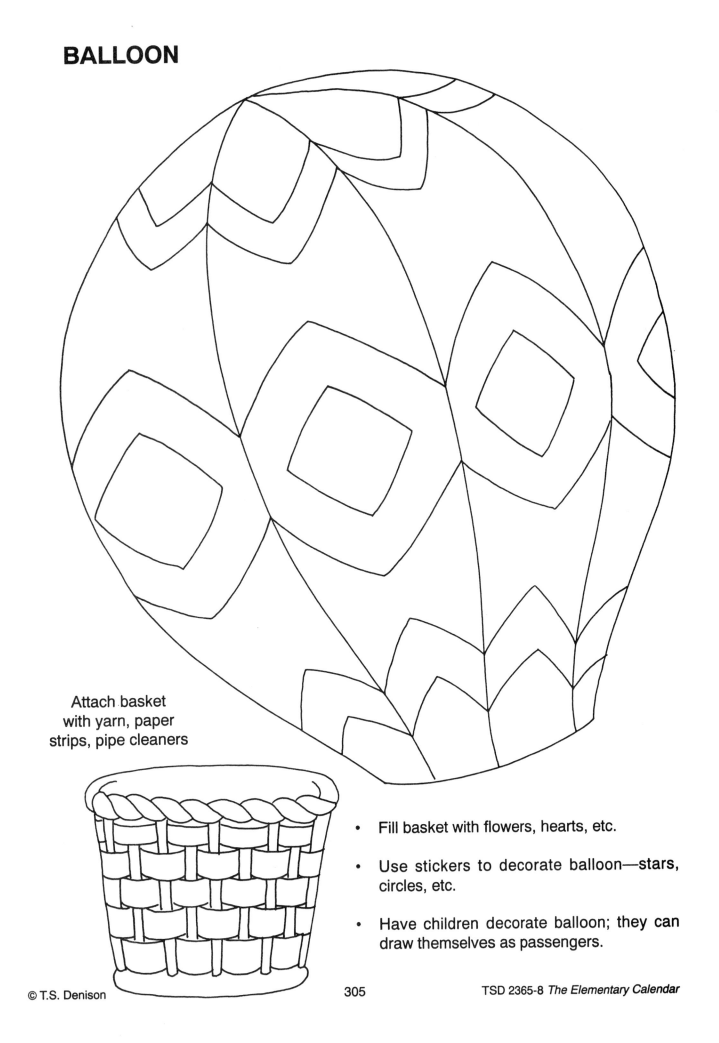

Attach basket
with yarn, paper
strips, pipe cleaners

- Fill basket with flowers, hearts, etc.

- Use stickers to decorate balloon—stars, circles, etc.

- Have children decorate balloon; they can draw themselves as passengers.

TWIRLY BIRDS

Materials: colored paper, stapler, precut ¾" x 12" (20 x 305 mm) strips in lots of bright colors.

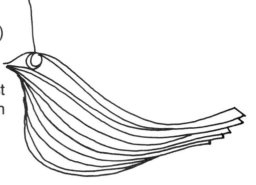

Select six strips and stack so that each added strip is at least ½" (13 mm) from the end of the one below it. Staple as shown leaving longer ends free.

Line up opposite ends evenly and staple.

Insert paper ring for eye and hang to move in the breeze.

FROG

Materials: 12" x 18" (305 x 420 mm) green paper, stapler, glue

Precut four 12" x ¾" (305 x 45 mm) strips from the end of 12" x 18" (305 x 457 mm) green paper. Cut the remaining paper into ¾" x 15" (20 x 390 mm) strips. For eyes, cut strips ¾" x 4½" (20 x 115 mm) and ¾" x 3" (20 x 76 mm).

Glue one ¾" x 15" (20 x 390 mm) strip into a ring for the body.

Glue or staple two ¾" x 12" (20 x 305 mm) strips at joining of body ring so that they stick straight out to each side. (This can be done in one step with a stapler.)

Bring the free ends of these 12" (305 mm) leg strips back under the body and glue, folding out an end for each foot. Dot glue between leg and body as shown. Fringe feet for "toes."

dot glue

Make rings from two 4½" (115 mm) and two 3" (76 mm) strips. Glue smaller ring inside larger and glue inside top of body ring (or try putting eyes on top of head).

M PUPPETS

Materials: 9" x 12" (229 x 305 mm) paper; scraps of yarn, paper and found materials

1. Fold the paper in thirds the long way, over-lapping slightly.
2. Fold paper in half, end to end, with the seam outside.
3. Fold each end back to the fold, on each side.

Insert thumb in one end opening, finger in the other.

Decorate puppets with scraps of yarn, paper, and found materials.

fingers

thumb

1 – orange   5 – green
2 – yellow   6 – white
3 – light blue   7 – red
4 – blue   8 – light brown

TSD 2365-8 *The Elementary Calendar*

Appendix

WORLD MAP

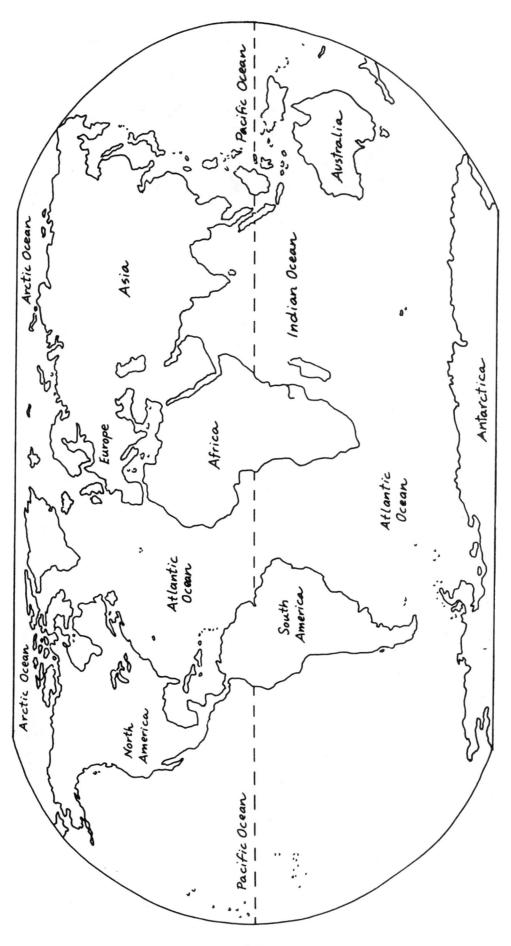

WORLD MAP

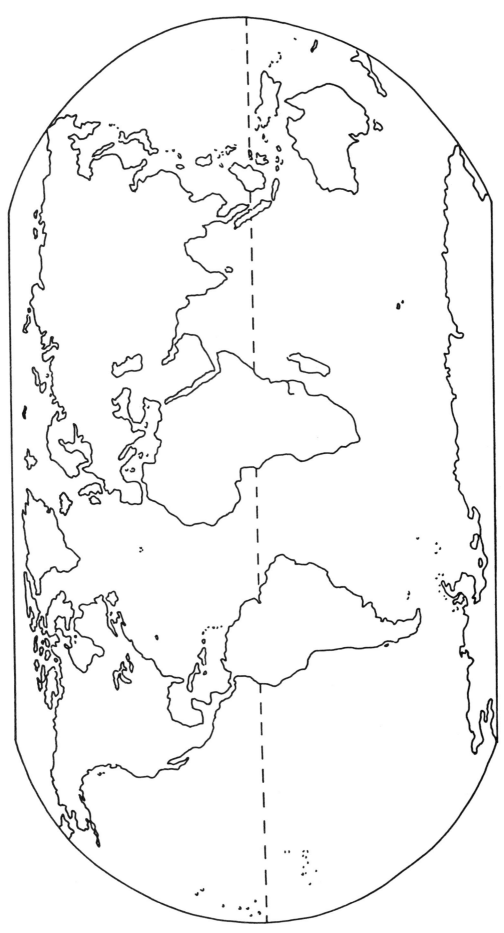

TSD 2365-8 *The Elementary Calendar*

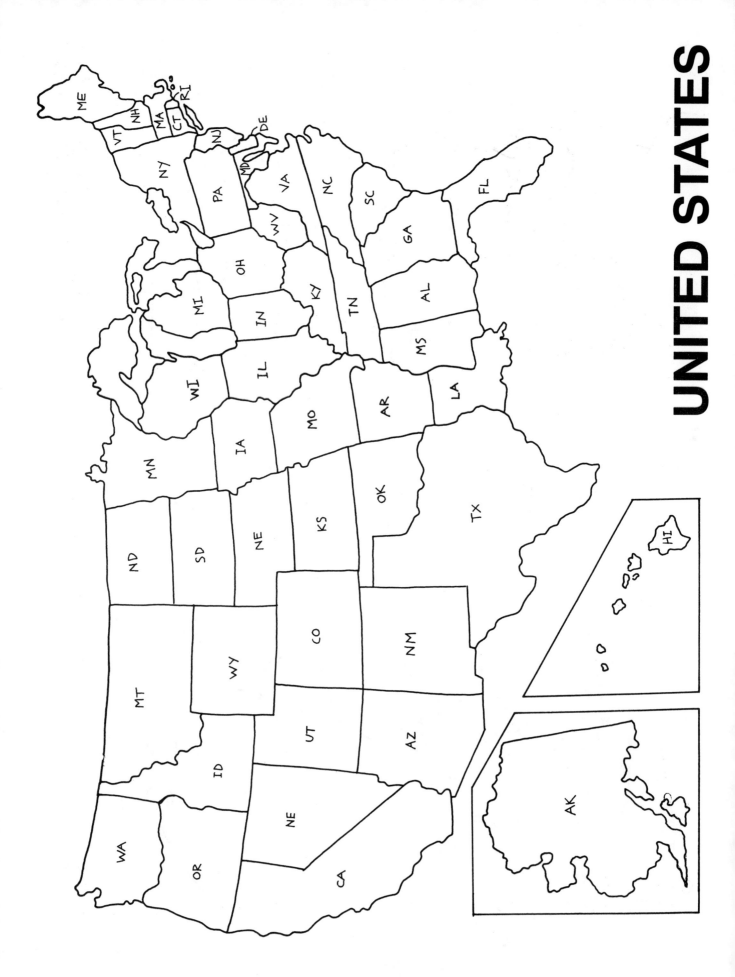

UNITED STATES

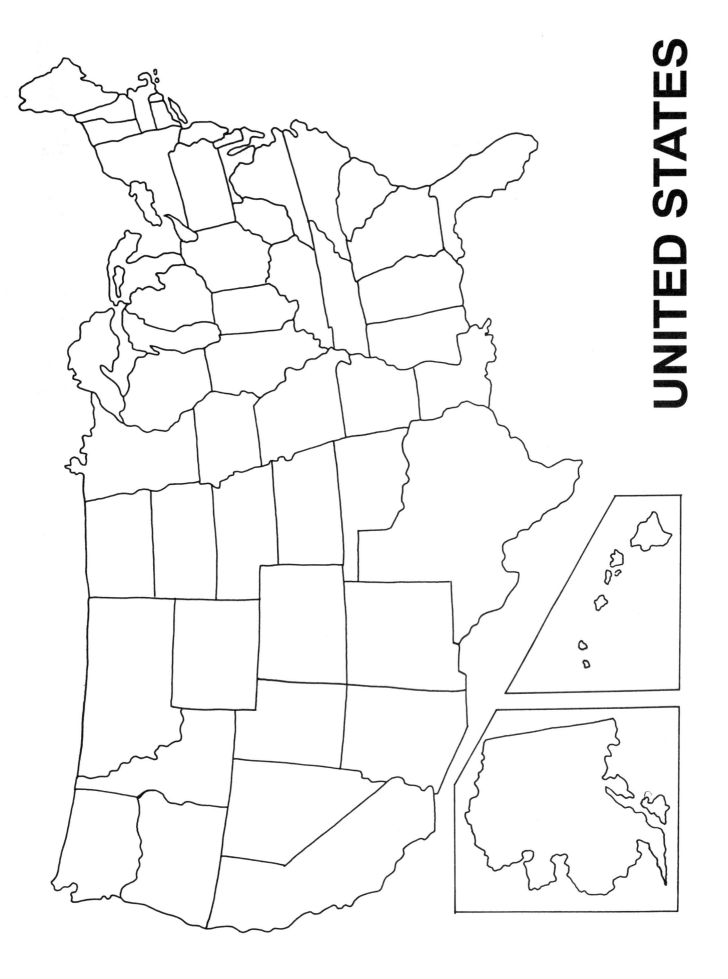

STATE STUFF

NAME	CAPITAL	NICKNAME	FLOWER	BIRD	TREE
ALABAMA	Montgomery	Heart of Dixie	camelia	yellowhammer	southern pine
ALASKA	Juneau	The Last Frontier, Land of Midnight Sun	forget-me-not	willow ptarmigan	Sitka spruce
ARIZONA	Phoenix	Grand Canyon State	Saguaro cactus flower	cactus wren	paloverde
ARKANSAS	Little Rock	Land of Opportunity	apple blossom	mockingbird	pine
CALIFORNIA	Sacramento	Golden State	golden poppy	California valley quail	California redwood
COLORADO	Denver	Centennial State	Rocky Mountain columbine	lark bunting	Colorado blue spruce
CONNECTICUT	Hartford	Constitution State	mountain laurel	robin	white oak
DELAWARE	Dover	The First State, The Diamond State	peach blossom	blue hen chicken	American holly
FLORIDA	Tallahassee	Sunshine State	orange blossom	mockingbird	sabal palmetto palm
GEORGIA	Atlanta	The Empire State of the South	Cherokee rose	brown thrasher	live oak
HAWAII	Honolulu	Aloha State	Hibiscus	nene (Hawaiian goose)	Kukui
IDAHO	Boise	Gem State	syringa	mountain bluebird	Western white pine
ILLINOIS	Springfield	The Prairie State	native violet	cardinal	white oak
INDIANA	Indianapolis	Hoosier State	peony	cardinal	tulip tree (yellow poplar)
IOWA	Des Moines	Hawkeye State	wild rose	Eastern goldfinch	oak
KANSAS	Topeka	Sunflower State	sunflower	Western meadowlark	cottonwood
KENTUCKY	Frankfort	Bluegrass State	goldenrod	cardinal	Kentucky coffee tree
LOUISIANA	Baton Rouge	Pelican State	magnolia	Eastern brown pelican	bald cypress
MAINE	Augusta	Pine Tree State	white pinecone and tassel	chickadee	eastern white pine
MARYLAND	Annapolis	Old Line State, Free State	black-eyed Susan	Baltimore oriole	white oak
MASSACHUSETTS	Boston	Bay State	mayflower	chickadee	American elm
MICHIGAN	Lansing	Wolverine State, Great Lake State	apple blossom	robin	white pine
MINNESOTA	Saint Paul	North Star State	pink and white lady's slipper	common loon	Norway or red pine
MISSISSIPPI	Jackson	Magnolia State	magnolia	mockingbird	magnolia

NAME	CAPITOL	NICKNAME	FLOWER	BIRD	TREE
MISSOURI	Jefferson City	Show Me State	hawthorn	bluebird	dogwood
MONTANA	Helena	Treasure State, Big Sky Country	bitterroot	Western meadowlark	ponderosa pine
NEBRASKA	Lincoln	Cornhusker State	goldenrod	Western meadowlark	western cottonwood
NEVADA	Carson City	Silver State, Sagebrush State	sagebrush	mountain bluebird	bristlecone pine and single-leaf piñon
NEW HAMPSHIRE	Concord	Granite State	purple lilac	purple finch	white birch
NEW JERSEY	Trenton	Garden State	purple violet	Eastern goldfinch	red oak
NEW MEXICO	Santa Fe	Land of Enchantment	yucca	roadrunner	piñon
NEW YORK	Albany	Empire State	rose	bluebird	sugar maple
NORTH CAROLINA	Raleigh	Tar Heel State, Old North State	dogwood	cardinal	pine
NORTH DAKOTA	Bismarck	Flickertale State, Peace Garden State, Sioux State	wild prairie rose	Western Meadowlark	American elm
OHIO	Columbus	Buckeye State	scarlet carnation	cardinal	buckeye
OKLAHOMA	Oklahoma City	Sooner State	mistletoe	scissor-tailed flycatcher	redbud
OREGON	Salem	Beaver State	Oregon grape	Western meadowlark	Douglas fir
PENNSYLVANIA	Harrisburg	Keystone State	mountain laurel	ruffed grouse	hemlock
RHODE ISLAND	Providence	Ocean State, Little Rhody	violet	Rhode Island Red	red maple
SOUTH CAROLINA	Columbia	Palmetto State	yellow jessamine	Carolina wren	palmetto
SOUTH DAKOTA	Pierre	Sunshine State, Coyote State	pasque flower	ring-necked pheasant	Black Hills spruce
TENNESSEE	Nashville-Davidson	Volunteer State	iris	mockingbird	tulip poplar
TEXAS	Austin	Lone Star State	bluebonnet	mockingbird	pecan
UTAH	Salt Lake City	Beehive State	sego lily	sea gull	blue spruce
VERMONT	Montpelier	Green Mountain State	red clover	hermit thrush	sugar maple
VIRGINIA	Richmond	Old Dominion	dogwood	cardinal	dogwood
WASHINGTON	Olympia	Evergreen State	Western rhododendron	willow goldfinch	western hemlock
WEST VIRGINIA	Charleston	Mountain State	rhododendron	cardinal	sugar maple
WISCONSIN	Madison	Badger State	wood violet	robin	sugar maple
WYOMING	Cheyenne	Equality State, Cowboy State	Indian paintbrush	meadowlark	cottonwood

United States Presidents

1. George Washington
   (1789–1797)
2. John Adams
   (1797–1801)
3. Thomas Jefferson
   (1801–1809)
4. James Madison
   (1809–1817)
5. James Monroe
   (1817–1825)
6. John Quincy Adams
   (1825–1829)
7. Andrew Jackson
   (1829–1837)
8. Martin Van Buren
   (1837–1841)
9. William Henry Harrison*
   (3/4–4/4 1841)
10. John Tyler
    (1841–1845)
11. James Knox Polk
    (1845–1849)
12. Zachary Tyler*
    (1849–1850)
13. Millard Fillmore
    (1850–1853)
14. Franklin Pierce
    (1853–1857)

15. James Buchanan
    (1857–18610
16. Abraham Lincoln**
    (1861–1865)
17. Andrew Johnson
    (1865–18690
18. Ulysses S. Grant
    (1869–1877)
19. Rutherford B. Hayes
    (1877–1881)
20. James A. Garfield**
    (3/4–9/19 1881)
21. Chester A. Arthur
    (1881–1885)
22. Grover Cleveland
    (1885–1889)
23. Benjamin Harrison
    (1889–1893)
24. Grover Cleveland
    (1893–1897)
25. William McKinley**
    (1897–1901)
26. Theodore Roosevelt
    (1901–1909)
27. William H. Taft
    (1909–1913)
28. Woodrow Wilson
    (1913–1921)

29. Warren G. Harding*
    (1921–1923)
30. Calvin Coolidge
    (1923–1929)
31. Herbert Hoover
    (1929–1933)
32. Franklin D. Roosevelt*
    (1933–1945)
33. Harry S. Truman
    (1945–1953)
34. Dwight D. Eisenhower
    (1953–1961)
35. John F. Kennedy**
    (1961–1963)
36. Lyndon B. Johnson
    (1963–1969)
37. Richard M. Nixon
    (1969–1974)
38. Gerald R. Ford
    (1974–1977)
39. James Earl Carter
    (1977–1981)
40. Ronald Reagan
    (1981–1989)
41. George Bush
    (1989–1992)
42. William Clinton
    (1992–   )

*   died in office
** assassinated

ANIMAL FAMILIES

ANIMAL	MOTHER	FATHER	BABY
bear	sow	boar	cub
cattle	cow	bull	calf; heifer (female)
cat	she-cat	tom-cat	kitten
chicken	hen	rooster	chick, cockerel (male); pullet (female)
deer	doe	buck; stag	fawn
dog	bitch	hound	puppy
duck	duck	drake	duckling
elephant	cow	bull	calf
fox	vixen	vix	cub, kit
goat	nanny	billy	kid
goose	goose	gander	gosling
horse	mare	stallion	foal
kangaroo	flyer	boomer	joey
lion	lioness	lion	cub
pig	sow	boar	farrow, shoat
rabbit	doe	buck	bunny, kit
seal	cow	bull	pup, cub
sheep	ewe	ram	lamb, lambkin; cosset
swan	pen	cob	cygnet
tiger	tigress	tiger	cub
turkey	hen	tom; gobbler	poult
whale	cow	bull	calf
wolf	bitch	dog wolf	cub, whelp

AND ALL TOGETHER . . .

A (an) ...	of . . .	A (an) . . .	of . . .
colony	ants	kindle	kittens
shrewdness	apes	exhalation, bevy	larks
sloth, sleuth	bears	pride	lions
swarm	bees	troop, tribe	monkeys
army	caterpillars	watch	nightingales
clowder	cats	parliament	owls
drove, herd	cattle	herd	pigs
flock, peep	chickens	ostentation, muster	peacocks
murder	crows	colony	penguins
heard	deer	string	ponies
pack	dogs	litter	pups
brace, paddling (on water), team (in flight)	ducks	bevy	quail
		crash, herd	rhinoceroses
convocation	eagles	nest, warren	rabbits
clutch	eggs	unkindness	ravens
herd	elephants	pod, crash, herd	seals
gang	elks	flock	sheep
business	ferrets	host	sparrows
charm	finches	dray	squirrels
school, shoal, run	fish	chattering, murmuration, congregation	starlings
skulk, earth	foxes	wedge, bevy, lamentation	swans
gaggle (on water), wedge, skein (in flight)	geese	knot	toads
		flock, rafter	turkeys
trip	goats	bale	turtles
brood	hens	school, gam, pod, shoal	whales
drift	hogs	rout(e), pack	wolves
herd, stable	horses	herd	zebras
troop, mob	kangaroos		

TSD 2365-8 *The Elementary Calendar*